GOD, THE WOMAN AND THEIR ENEMY

GOD, THE WOMAN AND THEIR ENEMY

JOSEPH BRICE

BRICE

Contents

Copyright

Dedication

While working on this project, I realize how much it takes for two people to become one. I have truly learned so much in the 3 ½ years of sacrifice to achieve this goal. Greater than a partner and more than support, my wife Janet has proven to believe in me and what I am called to do. Unselfish and sacrificial, you have been in helping to make this book come to fruition. Without a doubt, you are loyal, faithful, dedicated and devoted to your God, to me and your family. You are my Proverbs 31 woman, a beautiful person inside and out; your heart speaks volumes and has become my long-awaited treasure. I love you and thank you!

Acknowledgment

I would like to acknowledge the Kingdom Rights family and my community of believers; there are no other people quite like you. To the kingdom family of God, Christ, and Holy Spirit.

Howard Cottman, who stuck with me closer than a brother. You are truly a God send...thanks for all you have done and do.

Shakia Quickley who would believe you would come this far. Thank you for your support and undying commitment.

Geneva Cottman the newest of additions to the family but true to the cause and a loving support of the mission. Thank you.

Richard and Sandra Eular, you have been so instrumental to our vision. God use you as a sign for us in our move in 2020. Your obedience to God encouraged us even more to move forward and not back up with our vision in what would be the most challenging in modern day history. Thank you.

To all the supervisors, editors, proofreaders, publishers, graphic arts, web designers, marketing and all who were involved in making this project possible. Thank you for your intense labor.

From the Author

Woman...you are God's masterpiece, be who you are created to be; anything else is a cheap copy of your original. God's focus is your purpose...it should be yours too.

Some people are in your life to help you achieve your purpose, while others are assigned to you to destroy your purpose, kill your dreams and ultimately your life...

There are people who always count on you being there for them, but you can never count on them being there for you...make them accountable or let us not count at all.

Selfish has a face...

"When love is on trial, God is the only one qualified to judge it."

Joseph Brice

About the Author

Joseph Brice is the founding and senior pastor of Kingdom Rights Church in Birmingham, Alabama. His driving passion is presenting the Kingdom of God to those hungry and thirsty for God and those that may have never known it in the first place. Joseph Brice aims to raise awareness of the divine opportunity to be more than members of a church, but also be sons and daughters of the church. He stresses the importance of understanding and knowing your rights after becoming citizens of His kingdom. Brice is a speaker, builder, husband, and father. He lives in Birmingham with his wife, Janet, and their two daughters, Cianilyz and Briché.

PREFACE

I

Chapter 1: Irreplaceable

I am a Master!

I am the Master of the fallen angels and demons; they are my slaves; they do all the dirty jobs; they put in the work that I'm too sophisticated to do because I usually don't get my hands dirty unless it's the special cases! For I call the shots... any and everything that is unrighteous, hateful, deceitful, evil, and wicked is under my authority! I am the "fivefold terror," who rules all of those who love themselves and material things more than life!

Satan is my right hand, and he's my alter ego! It is to him that I have chosen I will give a son. But I must stop! For I *am* Lucifer, Satan, the Devil, the Serpent, and the False Prophet! These are all me... for I am the Multiple! Y'all don't know me? Ha! I was God's greatest work! I was "The Sun of the Morning!"—that feeling you get with a beautiful new day, well, that was I! I was, "The Bright and Morning Star!" Yes, that was me! I *am* Lucifer, the Morning Star! Y'all don't know me? I'm the power of the past. I use the past to destroy your future, and then I make it almost impossible to forget the past because my best days are behind me, but I can't let everybody know this about me.

I am Lucifer, and I do not work in the trenches! That is beneath me; I send Satan (my alter ego) and my crew to you! They do all of my dirty work, so I may be free to manipulate and arrange other demises. You have no clue as to what I am! I used to run the universe! You think you're something with your little positions? Yes, that's right, those little positions of power you have and talking about power? I had power! I was entrusted with God's power! I was like God, and I *was* a God! I was the next best thing to being God. But my "ego" wouldn't let me be happy with being second; because I want to be number one! I *gotta* be number one, like a hit record. After all, who wants to be the number two hit or album in the country? This goes across the board. I am ego, so I am full of pride!

No one is more arrogant than I am! I was personally taught by the Great that *I am*! No one could even come close to who I was... not even close! But pride got me into trouble! I had it all, yet I wanted more. Is more even possible? Well, when I looked at The Most High God, I wanted to take His place; I wanted to be Him and wanted Him to know what it feels like to be me. Well, He's always been at the top, and I wanted to know what that feels like, to be number one! Now don't act like you don't know what I'm talking about. I have many of you working for me right now, trying to get to the top, and I know you're willing to sell your soul to get there! We're keeping it real! After all, this is what started the first war in Heaven... fighting to be on the top; pride and greed!

I really thought I had God and Heaven on lock—I thought

I was irreplaceable! So many of you think like me because you *are* me! I am so selfish. I sacrificed the entire kingdoms for my wants and desires. I couldn't see beyond what I wanted. I started the first competition in Heaven. There had never been competition there before, but we all worked together to complete the vision.

I knew some would get hurt, but that's the price I was willing for them to pay. I am so valuable that God would not dare do anything to me! In fact, I thought God couldn't make it without me! Because I think of myself as God—I am God's replacement, this is my dream! I want to be Him! And while I was working on my plan to be number one, God was MIA, or at least that's what I thought. It seemed as though He put everything He owned in my hands and was giving me space to do my thing. I was accustomed to running most things, anyway! So I was going for it! It was during this time when everything changed.

We all discovered later, too late, that God was down in the second Heaven working on a new thing, a new project. We all hung out in the third Heaven—this is where God lives! It was the place to be, the King's Court. Until that fateful day when God called that meeting, I will never forget it! I was wondering, "What can this be about?" God began to tell me about my pride, secret meetings, and the iniquity in my heart! I tried to defend myself, but the more I talked, the more I lied! You will find that God does not handle being lied to very well! He stripped me of my authority, beauty, and glory, but surprisingly allowed me to keep my talents, gifts, and anointing! I couldn't believe He allowed me to keep anything!

Then he threw me out! Can you believe this? He cast me

down out of His kingdom! This is the beginning of my end. And as I was falling, I was transforming into something else.

When God is ready, He will reveal what is already here; he will reveal the answer. When it comes to intelligence of that infinite level, trust this: the answer always comes before the question. If we can think of a question, know that the answer was first just hidden from us until the time came to reveal it. We call it discovery and inventions. God gives man the knowledge, skills, and abilities; this is what makes us like Him. How we use these gifts determines if we are like Him or them, "the fallen angels."

It is the same for truth and lies. A lie comes from a twisted truth, but truth cannot come from a twisted lie. Why? Because the truth was first and always will be here long after the lie dissipates. Remember, Lucifer started out good as well but did not endure to the end. Understand this, you can be anointed and not have God, but you cannot have God's glory without having Him. The anointing is a gift from God, but the "Glory" is God! The anointing is a gift to use in life for life, and on the other hand, the Glory *is* life. Many of us don't understand this difference and are impressed with those who are simply anointed.

Y'all don't know me! I was God's greatest work! I was entrusted with God's power! I was like God. I *was* a God! I was the next best thing to being God. Lucifer, Satan, that Old Devil, the Serpent (Dragon), the False Prophet. Lucifer; he was the greatest living creature besides God Himself. He was created for this purpose. He was the CEO of Heaven, but of course, God is the Originator, Creator, Founder, and Owner. So Lucifer got demoted; he was thrown down out of Heaven by reason of betrayal and treason. He organized a rebellion against the Kingdom of God. He broke the laws that the kingdom was established on. He took it upon himself to try to overthrow the kingdom. The Serpent is Lucifer's degenerate state. Because of how cunning and deceptive he had become, he was made into a snake.

Lucifer was a prince, a ruler in Heaven. He fell with a vengeance. He was stripped of his heavenly kingdom authority. When he was cast down, he still had his training and education concerning government or kingdom order. My "ego" wouldn't let me be happy with being second. I want to be number one! I gotta *be* number one! Like a hit record, who wants to be the number two hit or album in the country? This goes across the board. I *am* ego! No one is more arrogant than I am! I was personally taught by the best, "the Great I am!" No one could even come close to who I was... not even close! Pride got me into trouble! I had it all but wanted more. Is more even possible? Funny, I was never satisfied.

Well, when I looked at "The Most High God" I wanted to take His place. I wanted to be Him and wanted Him to know what it feels like to be me. Well, He's always been at the top! I wanted to know what it feels like to be number one! Well, don't act like you don't know what I'm talking about. I have many of you working for me right now, trying to go to the top, and you're willing to sell your soul to get there! When you are willing to do anything to be on top, I'm your source.

This is what started the first war in Heaven; fighting to be at the top; pride and greed! Not being satisfied with my purpose. I really thought I had God and Heaven on lock. I thought I was irreplaceable! So many of you think like me because you *are* me! We are family. Where my GOATS at?

I am so selfish that I sacrificed the entire kingdom for my wants and desires. I couldn't see beyond what I wanted. I knew some would get hurt, but that's the price I was willing for them to pay. I am so valuable; God would not dare do anything to me! I thought God couldn't make it without me because I think of myself as God. I see myself replacing God. This is my dream! I want to be Him! While I was working on my plan to be number one, God was MIA, or at least that's what I thought. It seemed as though He was giving me space to do my thing. I was running everything anyway! So I was going for it! It was during this time when everything changed. We all discovered later, too late, that God was down in the second Heaven, working on a new thing, a new project. We all hung out in the third Heaven, and this is where God lives! Now that was the spot, the club! When God called that meeting, I will never forget it! I was wondering, "What can this be about?" God began to tell me about my pride, secret meetings, and the iniquity in my heart! I tried to defend myself, but the more I talked, the more I lied! You will find God does not handle being lied to very well!

I wonder what God will do now without me. This is the beginning of my end. As I was falling, I began transforming into something else. I don't know what this was. It was ugly, and I am not happy about it... somebody is gonna pay! So no matter how we look at it, we all are a part of a kingdom and family. God's family is the original, and the split of that kingdom is why we battle so much here on earth. The kingdom of light or kingdom of darkness, forces for good or evil, love or lust, love or hate. No matter how many businesses, or families, governments, armies, entertainers, or worship houses... there are only two kingdoms. The Serpent is working for his boss, Lucifer, and he represents wisdom and cunningness. He has mastered giving what we want in exchange for pleasure and him ruling our lives and being the center of our worship. Be careful and attentive during any kind of worship, so you know what you are worshiping and know if it's of God.

The Serpent, who is he, and what is he? He is the greatest enemy the Woman will ever have. Temper is his character, his purpose, and his fallen position. He made his debut along with the Woman in Heaven (eternity). In the beginning, when Eve was in the Garden, he was the sly and wise Serpent. He's the smooth-talker. He talked her right out of her home; her husband, children, and the good, secure life she had known. She had it all, and somehow he made her feel she was missing something. The truth is, he robbed her! He befriended her and gained her trust. Then he took away her trust with her God and her husband. He offered her power and authority equal to God, but there's no such thing, so he lied.

We all need to find our lane, our purpose for life, and stay in it. Here you will find the Serpent again, but now in time. You will see that he laid low until God made the Woman. He had no interest in the man; it was the Woman who he wanted. He knows if he has the Woman, he has everything. She is the source of life and the producer of life. She's God's partner for life. She sets the tone for the home. She is the foundation that all things are built on.

The mystery of the Woman, it seems so simple yet complicated, because she doesn't know who she is. If she will allow a man to pimp her, then why not pimp herself? I know I need you for the job, but I am not willing to pay you what you are worth. I fear you will show that glory that I don't have but need to win.

Your enemy's job is to rob you of your identity, then he gains ownership, and then he'll have your confidence. He needs your power, and in return, he'll give you some authority. But oh, the Woman is already powerful and has authority! Again, she just doesn't know it. When you don't understand this, then you listen to your enemy, the Serpent, and use your God-given talents and power to give power to your enemy, the Satan. Then he uses it against you to break up the home, business, marriage, or start a war.

Satan needs you! He is nothing without you! Listen to the voice inside you; is it the voice of good or evil? Are you building a life or tearing it down? Where do we think the songwriter is getting his material? Who's the inspiration for the playwright or screenplays? Yes, she has a voice, but mostly behind the scenes. Where are your royalties, O! Royal One of The Most High? The harsh reality is that the Woman is Lucifer's replacement!

II

Chapter 2: The Masterpiece

She is the greatest of all God's creations; a Masterpiece.

The Woman was created from the start to be a problem solver. She was created out of necessity! She was created with much thought and great passion, much patience, many talents, and gifts, much love... in fact, the greatest love of all! She was envisioned, she was fashioned, and she was created with God's heart and mind!

Imagine being betrayed by your closest friend, or companion, spouse, partner, mother, father, children, job, or religion—by anyone to whom you gave your heart. Now, put all of this betrayal together and try to go to work and be productive. Well, this is what makes the woman "the great wonder!" For God created her when He was in His greatest pain! God fashioned her while He was hurting; when He had still allowed Lucifer to be in charge! God sacrificed His happiness for the good of His Kingdom—His Heaven. "The Most

High God" was feeling low! "The Most Exalted One" was feeling weak! "The Self Existing One" was hurting and in pain. He never knew hurt before this. His heart was breaking into innumerable pieces. And with a broken heart, God stepped down into the second Heaven. Remember, His home is in the third Heaven, far above everything in creation and the galaxies. For He lives in eternity, which is timeless.

After Lucifer's betrayal and scheming to take over, God's trust in him was damaged forever! But Lucifer had a secret: he was jealous of God.

God, who is his Master and Creator. He was jealous of the One who made him. He wanted everything that God had, including His life. He wanted God's plan and vision. He wanted the glory and credit for all of God's work.

Can you imagine a person who admires you and claims to love you but actually envies you and hates you at the same time?

People of power could not have the power they possess if it had not been given to them from Heaven above! For God is the distributor of power! Just as He gave Lucifer this power, which he misused, we do the same on earth. Now Lucifer is God's SECOND greatest creation. I emphasize this because most people do not know or have a clue as to how the Woman came into existence!

The story goes that the safety of Heaven was in danger, and no one but God knew this. The plan was not written on paper, but in Lucifer's heart. This is why God judges the heart alone, and men judge the outer appearance, which is shallow and thus ungodly.

God could see Lucifer's hate for Him, his jealousy, his

murderous plot, and his hostile takeover! Now pay attention! God, being aware of Lucifer's plan, thought it was imperative that He do something about it, "but what?" This is where we all should really have respect for God. For this is way before our existence as human beings; this is the account of Heaven's dilemma.

Trouble started there first; it is trouble's place of origin. Get this picture: Lucifer is God's partner, and he was created out of God's "creative genius." God created Lucifer out of love. But something had gone wrong along the way. You can have a child out of a loving relationship, and when that child gets older, all of a sudden, they change, and it can seem as though you don't even know your own child. The same can happen in a marriage, leaving you to ask yourself, "Who is this person next to me?" I'm giving you these parallels to take away this fantasy and deception that religion has birthed Satan.

Everything has an origin, "Eternity is before time." Know this: Lucifer is God's creation, created to serve Him; this is his assignment. By serving God, he is not doing God a favor—it's his job; it's what he was created for. It is similar to the movie *I, Robot*, in which the robot was made to serve, not have its own mind. Think about it, where did the writers get this idea for a movie? It came from Above because God is trying to tell us something along our journey.

Why do we have so many movies and even comic books from back in the day where the storyline is always about a battle between good and evil? Someone is always trying to take over the world with evil intent. There's always someone going against the natural order of things.

Who is the true author of these stories? It's the Ruler of

Heaven who is with us all along. Coming back to our story, now God was hurting and needed to do something. If He destroyed Lucifer because of what He knew, it would appear that God had lost His mind, and Heaven would be in an uproar! For no one in the Heaven had ever known fear or death before this.

They had never experienced an argument or disagreement because whatever God says, it's done; whatever He desires, it's fulfilled.

Lucifer was loved like a mother, a brother, and a sister because these are not gendered relations but beings of love. These are beings that have gifts and talents for good living and happiness. Lucifer was and continues to be the most talented, the most intelligent, the most beautiful, the most respected being of manifestation ever created! He is everything! He is in charge of all the "feel goods" of Heaven. This is why we love to be entertained; it makes us "feel good!"

Heaven is just a beautiful place. Like a never-ending wedding day, there is always just joy and peace, where everyone's happy. But it was only a matter of time before Lucifer acted on what was in his heart. Lucifer was the being that the angels were supposed to respect and follow by God's design. They awaited his instructions like little children, depending on their mother for the day to begin. God had made Lucifer everything to them.

But remember, God is spirit, and Lucifer is a tangible, manifested being! He ruled from a throne! He was royalty, not like kings of the earth who go to war for spoils to gain riches, but he was created rich! He knew nothing else but principalities and powers; he knew the kingdom!

That's why it's ridiculous for us to be divided over race, religion, denominations, orientations, and any other distractions. The true battle is about the kingdom! We use these things as the drive to our purposes demonstrated through hate or love, but it all started with the Divine kingdom, and that's where it will end. Satan is the fallen angel from the Kingdom of Heaven, and he knows the power and glory of that kingdom! He exercises the authority given to him, and even in his wrongdoings, he does not abandon the principles of the kingdom. These principles are the truth that can't be undone, as the law of gravity, which is not biased or prejudiced. It works for anyone and everyone, whether you believe in it or not. Believing is a benefit to us. These things are in place for a reason and, more than less, for our own good.

Where do our emotions, our feelings, and our challenges come from? Does it all generate from within us? No. This is bigger than all of us, and it all comes down to the war that started in Heaven, and we must come to grips with this!

We are in a time where knowledge is increasing rapidly, then why shouldn't God share revelations with us? Why should His children be in the dark? The world is dark enough. We can be the lights of the world. But where do we get the strength to go on when all seems to fail? How do we succeed? I tell you, it's the kingdom, it's the Creator in us, the characteristics of the Father of the Kingdom.

Hence God came up with a plan. For the sake of His children (in this case, angels). He would not expose Lucifer and his plot of evil. Now at that time, Lucifer was God's greatest work. His hit song, His best record, His top model, His best movie, His greatest athlete, His greatest novel, His greatest business, and known success! Could God top this? He stepped down into the second Heaven and humbled Himself to His own very beginnings. He went to work, yet again, on His greatest hit! His best and greatest creation ever!

He remembered His lonely days of having a dream. Yes, even God has dreams! Where did you think dreaming originated from? He stepped away from praise, He stepped away from glory, and He stepped away from the center of attraction. He went to work while in pain. "If you want what you've never had, you must be willing to do what you've never done." Thus, God was hurt and working through His pain.

Does this sound familiar? "There's nothing new under the sun, what is, already has been." He could not share His plan with anyone. He couldn't trust anyone this time. This vision was so grand, and God just needed to get it out of Him right away. He was working with God's speed! This creation that was brand new, how will it be received, He thought? So He worked and hurt and hurt and worked. He couldn't stop! Heaven wondered what was going on, but God wouldn't expose His plan. On the other hand, there was also a secret taking place in the works of Lucifer.

Lucifer spoke to the angels about things that were contrary to what God gave him to do. Some of the angels were reluctant to obey his orders because they know God and how He is so particular about order and protocol. Some were convinced that it was okay to deviate a little because Lucifer was in charge in the absence of God. But what they didn't know is that Lucifer was playing on words and slightly and gradually making changes to the order—the Laws and Order that God has put in place. This is the first case of an opportunist at work, taking advantage of the situation while violating the trust God has in him.

Where Lucifer thought that he could get away with his conspiracy, God already knew of it because He can read the heart. The heart speaks to God even when the mouth is shut, but here's the deal, no one knows this, but God. Lucifer was so arrogant and full of himself that he really believed he was irreplaceable. The truth of the matter is that Heaven was run like a kingdom, but its essence lay in the feel of a household, for the most part, with all the amenities imaginable. It is an environment of love, and God is the "Loving Dictator," like a parent. Therefore, when Lucifer was recruiting those to rebel, revolutionizing for a democracy, God kept watch because He had worked too hard to allow this takeover. But Lucifer, who is full of himself and pride, continued to plot. No matter how costly it was and how many lives were destroyed in his wake, Lucifer was blinded by his own ambitions.

Lucifer did not have any experience outside of Heaven's protected gates. He was full of untested ideas. He believed he had a better way of living, with him putting a great deal of focus on worship and position of power. He desired more and more worship and praise, solely for him. He is the physical being and material focus of all things worshiped. Little did he know that God was already at work on his replacement! Lucifer had been given so much love, authority, and power, but he took it for granted and believed himself to be irreplaceable! The thing is, his arrogance and pride became his downfall. Forgetting who made him and what he was made for, Lucifer was tripping.

While Lucifer was doing his thing and thinking that he

was getting away with it, God was engaged in His greatest work to date! He was working on something totally different from anything He had ever done before. He thought to Himself, "it's gotta be glorious, beautiful, graceful, strong but gentle in nature, talented, nurturing, supportive, dedicated, patient, loving, kind, passionate, confident, compassionate, emotional, and caring. It needs to be like Him but different, creative, adorable, irresistible, elegant, faithful, trustworthy, of godly character, creative, and a producer of life—a multi-faceted creature!'

Nothing that God had created up until this point was equipped to give life. This was it! It was similar to Lucifer but better! God had indeed outdone Himself!

He fashioned her from His glory and marveled at His creation, "She is equipped with the makings of giving life." To this point, God and His word created everything. Life was produced by what He said. Now, this new creation was gifted with the hidden ability to produce life from its body! This had never been done before!

"This is impeccable, flawless, perfect, unblemished, spotless, faultless, immaculate...wow! What is it, what do we call it?" He answered Himself, "Woman!"

This was God's best work to date, but no one was there to see. Only the stars and planets were His witnesses. Then He looked at her and thought, "She is formed but without life!" So God filled her with His Own Spirit, and she became a living soul!

She is WOMAN! She represents the beginning of healing God's broken heart. She brings Him unspeakable joy! She's alive and facing her Creator... She is beautiful and Innocent.

When He created Lucifer, He dressed him in a coat of diamonds, similar to a bride's gown with a train. The coat would give off this glorious and radiant illumination! It would fill the place with a feeling. Anyone would know when that glory was in the room!

Now for this newest creation, God posed the question, "Could she surpass Lucifer's glory?" He thought, "She must!" Until now, the Heavens never knew of competition. This had become the first official competition! While she stood in her wardrobe, she came into herself and realized her creation had a purposeful meaning. Due to the circumstances, she had a natural competitive edge to her. "How should we dress her? She is different, no doubt, but just the same, we want her to really stand out and be noticeably different without her saying a word. Just her presence will fill the place wherever and whenever she enters."

"She must be glorious with Godlike qualities...she is the other Me! She's naked without shame and is not ashamed; she's a natural beauty! She's everything, but how do we dress her?" He thought "With Glory!" God gathered up the sun, the moon, and some stars for the occasion. He began to dress her because she is like Him, and must manifest what the Heavens has not yet seen. "Can she handle the greatest glory made available?" God began to dress her for the first time, and her garments had not been worn before... for such a creation was unheard of.

He took the sun in His hands and began to make a pattern like a seamstress to make her garment. He was excited at how she could handle the sun! God is the greatest light, and He made her of Himself; the next greatest light is the sun, and now she is wearing the sun! The sun is the light that rules the day, and this creature wore it like a coat! Then God placed the moon under her feet, which is the light that rules the night!

Then God looked at her and said, she must have a crown because "I have found my Queen." The Heavens had never had a Queen before...what a creation! God took the stars in His hands and began to make a crown with them! The crown was shaped and fitted to perfection. He then placed the crown made of 12 stars upon her head! She was wearing three parts of the glory that are used to make the universe.

The trinity of the universe was now on this new creation...she was wearing them! "Who is this?" After looking for the final inspection of His work, God sighed a sigh of relief and gratitude, plus a bit of satisfaction... "what a masterpiece!" God was more than satisfied with His work! It was amazing for God to have created such a masterpiece from His pain.

Created from pain, this very creature will surely endure pain. The Woman has inherited this creative ability and strength from her Maker, which is God! She is the epitome of beauty, majesty, and royalty! She bows to no one but her Maker and Creator! Now back to the third Heaven, no one is higher than Lucifer but God Himself. Wait a minute... There is another that the Heavens don't know about?

She was now ready for the angels of Heavens to see, but first, God had to go above and handle His business. He placed the Woman in the embrace of the second Heaven's universe for safe-keeping. Then God called a meeting and presented His finding. He asked Lucifer a number of questions. Lucifer suspected that one of his angels must have sold him out and told on him (a snitch). He had deceived, "one out three angels" on a twisted lie taken from God's truth. The Lord asked Lucifer about the iniquity that is in his heart. "How did this happen? When did this happen Lucifer?" God asked. "I've been good to you; how could you be so wicked?" The heart is like a womb; it's the birthplace for good or evil. The problem is, iniquity can't be God's baby, because there's no evil in God and nor can there be. Lucifer had been unfaithful and was pregnant with an evil thing, conceived by disobedience. His heart couldn't hide it any longer. It started to show! "This is treason and adultery!" The angels were shocked at the discovery, but not the betrayal. After all, Lucifer had tried to convert many to follow him in this evil plot to be God! He said, " I will set my throne above the throne of The Most High God!" Only to be cast down. God could have destroyed him, but He cast him down along with the angels who obeyed and followed him. "Be careful of who you are following!"

The earth has no clue as to what is about to take place. Lucifer and his followers have failed on their attempt for the kingdom takeover. Although God knows this He just has to establish evidence of this treason. These losers are sent to a holding place until the day these allegations will be judged. On their way down as fallen angels they see something absolutely mind blowing. It is extremely difficult for Lucifer to witness this site. As he was falling and losing his known beauty and majesty.

And there appeared a great wonder in Heaven; a woman clothed with the sun, and the moon under her feet, and upon her head a crown of twelve stars: and she being with child cried, travailing in birth, and pained to be delivered.

And there appeared another wonder in Heaven; a great red dragon, having seven heads and ten horns, and seven crowns upon his heads. And his tail drew the third part of the stars of Heaven, and did cast them to the earth: and the dragon stood before the Woman who was ready to be delivered, to devour her child as soon as it was born. Soon she brought forth a man-child, who was to rule all nations with a rod of iron: and her child was caught unto God, and to his throne. And the Woman fled into the wilderness, where she hath a place prepared by God that they should feed her there for a thousand two hundred and three score days (3-1/2 years).

And then there was a War in heaven: Michael and his angels fought against the dragon; and the dragon fought and his angels, and prevailed not; neither was their place found any more in Heaven. And the great dragon was cast out, that old Serpent, called the Devil, and Satan, which deceives the whole world: he was cast out into the earth, and his angels were cast out with him. And a loud voice was heard saying in Heaven, "Now is come salvation, and strength, and the kingdom of our God, and the power of his Christ: for the accuser of our brethren is cast down, which accused them before our God day and night. And they overcame him by the blood of the Lamb, and the word of their testimony; and they loved not their lives unto the death. Therefore, rejoice, ye Heavens, and ye that dwell in them. Woe to the inhabitants of the earth and the sea! For the Devil is come down unto you, having great wrath, because he knows that he hath a short time."

When the dragon saw he was cast unto the earth, he persecuted the Woman, which brought forth the man-child. And the Woman was given two wings of a great eagle, that she might fly into the wilderness, into her place, where she is nourished for a time, and times, and half a time, (3-1/2 years) from the face of the Serpent. And the Serpent cast out of his mouth water as a flood after the Woman, that he might cause her to be carried away of the flood. And the earth helped the Woman, and the earth opened her mouth, and swallowed up the flood, which the dragon cast out of his mouth. And the dragon was wroth with the Woman, so it went to make war with the remnant of her seed, which keeps the commandments of God, and have the testimony of Jesus Christ.

The Woman is without a doubt God's Masterpiece!

Now Lucifer the Serpent is coming to the earth with much hate and vengeance... beware!

III

Chapter 3: The Serpent

The Serpent misguides the Woman by coaxing her to eat the forbidden fruit...not so much just an "Apple" (which is symbolic), but through whatever takes her away from fulfilling her true purpose in life, which is to make this world a better place for all humanity.

Today his greatest fruit has become, "MONEY!" Now money is the voice and the way the Serpent speaks to us... so listen!

"Now, the Serpent was more cunning than any beast of the field which the Lord God had made. And he said to the Woman, "Yea, hath God said, 'Ye shall not eat of every tree of the garden'?" And the Woman said to the Serpent, "We may eat of the fruit of the trees of the Garden: but of the fruit of the tree, which is in the midst of the Garden, God hath said, 'Ye shall not eat of it, neither shall ye touch it, lest ye die'."

And so the Serpent said to the Woman, "Ye shall not surely die: For God doth know that in the day ye eat thereof, then your eyes shall be opened, and ye shall be as gods, knowing good and evil."

And when the Woman saw that the tree was good for food and that it was pleasant to the eyes, and that it was a tree to be desired to make one wise to eat from, she took the fruit thereof and ate it, and then she also gave to her husband with her; and he ate it as well. And the eyes of them both were opened, and they knew that they were naked. Upon this, they sewed fig leaves together and made themselves aprons. That's when they heard the voice of God walking in the Garden in the cool of the day, and Adam and his wife hid themselves from the presence of God amongst the trees of the Garden.

And the Lord God called unto Adam, and said unto him, "Where art thou?" And Adam replied, "I heard thy voice in the Garden, and I was afraid because I was naked; so I hid myself." And he said, "Who told thee that thou wast naked? Hast thou eaten of the tree, whereof I commanded thee that thou shouldest not eat?" And the man said, "the Woman, whom thou gavest to be with me, she gave me of the tree, and I did eat."

And so the Lord said unto the Woman, "What is this that thou hast done?" And the Woman said, "The Serpent beguiled me, and I did eat." And then God turned to the Serpent and said unto him, "Because thou hast done this, thou art cursed above all cattle, and above every beast of the field; upon thy belly shalt thou go, and dust shalt thou eat all the days of thy life. And I will put enmity between thee and the Woman, and between thy seed and her seed; it shall bruise thy head, and thou shalt bruise his heel."

Unto the Woman, He said, "I will greatly multiply thy sorrow and thy conception; in sorrow thou shalt bring forth children; and thy desire shall be to thy husband, and he shall rule over thee."

And unto Adam, He said, "Because thou hast hearkened unto the voice of thy wife, and hast eaten of the tree, of which I commanded thee, saying, thou shalt not eat of it: cursed is the ground for thy sake; in sorrow shalt thou eat of it all the days of thy life; thorns also and thistles shall it bring forth to thee; and thou shalt eat the herb of the field; in the sweat of thy face shalt thou eat bread, till thou return unto the ground; for out of it wast thou taken: for dust thou art, and unto dust shalt thou return."

Adam turned to his wife and called her Eve because she was the mother of all things living. Then God made coats of skins and clothed both Adam and Eve.

And God said, "Behold, the man is become as one of us, to know good and evil: and now, lest he put forth his hand, and take also of the tree of life, and eat, and live forever. Therefore, the Lord God sent him forth from the Garden of Eden, to till the ground from whence he was taken. So he drove out the man; and he placed at the east of the Garden of Eden Cherubim, and a flaming sword which turned every way, to keep the way of the tree of life."

In the beginning, when Eve was in the Garden, he was the sly and wise Serpent. He was the smooth-talker, and he talked her right out of her home, her husband, children, and the good, secure life she had known. She had it all, and somehow he made her feel she was missing something. The truth is, he robbed her! He befriended her, gained her trust, and then he took away her trust with God and with her husband.

He offered her power and authority equal to God. But there is no such thing...so, of course, he lied.

We all need to find our lane, our purpose for life, and stay in it. Here you will find the Serpent again, but in time, you will see that he laid low until God made the Woman. He had no interest in the man; it was the Woman who he wanted. He knows if he has the Woman, he has everything. She is the source for life, and she is life. She sets the tone for the home. She is the foundation on which all things are built. It seems so simple yet complicated because she doesn't know who she is. If she allows a man to pimp her, then why not sell her own body? Your enemy's job is to rob you of your identity, then he gains ownership, and then he'll have your confidence.

The Serpent had deceived the Woman, but when approached by God, she didn't lie. Do you know why? Because she is truth. She is no liar, but the Devil is. When she lies or lives a lie, it is not her nature but her enemy who's taken her mind and body over. No woman was born a whore, but was made into one. No woman was born a liar but was made into one. No woman was born a gold digger but was made into one. No woman was born evil but was made evil. Every Woman was born good and pure, but the sinful nature of that Serpent is always after her. The Woman needs help, trust, and belief that she will get it! In these last days of the countdown of evil and the revelation of the Anti-Christ, the Woman will be very strategic in how the prophecies will unfold. Nothing can happen without her. Satan needs her permission, and when it is not granted, he manipulates her and steals her glory. Lucifer misses his glory days, so he tries to relive them by attaching himself to the Woman.

Why does she continue to empower him? She doesn't need his help, but he needs hers, and her help is God and the earth. This is what she inherited from her Heavenly Father. The Serpent continues to lace lies with things that glitter. The Woman is intrigued with things that don't last when in reality, she is the everlasting Queen proclaimed in the Heavens before time. She is the owner of the glory, not a fake copy. The Devil is deceitful because she already owns everything he uses to entice her. Why is the earth called "her" in the Bible? Why is America called "the beautiful?" Why do we say "Mother Earth?" Because God already knew the end from the beginning, and it has never been about the Woman messing up, but about setting a trap for the greatest adversary ever..."Lucifer" AKA "Satan" AKA the "Devil"! The concealed ugliness in this beautiful angel's heart would not show itself until the creation of the Woman. It was her glory that exposed him because she was beautiful, inside and out! This is why the Devil attempts to make the Woman vain; because he knows from experience that outer beauty has limited power and will fade away, but inner beauty is everlasting and will never fade or be found in "shade!"

He knows that in Heaven—if the Woman makes it—she will be given unprecedented glory, laced with everlasting beauty, equal to her heart. God loves a beautiful heart! Lucifer's true feelings were hidden until the Woman's presence exposed him. Her very Godly glorified presence brought out things in him that he didn't even know about. He didn't know how hateful and prejudiced he was until he saw her.

Think about that; how many hateful acts have we experienced from an individual or group whom we didn't know personally? But they still abused you, all because it was something about you that they didn't like or agree with. This is how God exposes the evil in one's heart. Please understand; we are not wise enough to outsmart such a supreme being as God, who possesses unparalleled intelligence and wisdom. Know this also, Satan is a "control freak," and whatever he can't control, he will seek to destroy! Until the Woman was created, Lucifer thought he was holy and righteous because he did things supposedly for God and in the name of God. But this did not make him righteous. You see, this is called a form of Godliness! If you don't have love or haven't experienced the true love of God, the ritual will fool you. Without love, it's all for nothing, and God is not in it! Going to a worship service does not make us righteous; it does not make us Godly or worthy of God's love. She was given so much glory until her very presence stripped him of all of his glory. She blew his cover. Don't you understand now when the Devil says this is "why I hate the woman!" it is evident that God loves her.

"The heart is deceitful above all things, and it is desperately wicked: who can know it but God?" Lucifer was in Heaven acting like he loved God while hiding in his heart treason and treacherous evil that could only be displayed throughout countless generations in time. Every generation we've had and will see will expose a little more of the evil, which was hidden for so long. Every hidden secret is revealed because of the Woman. God uses her, like a beautiful instrument, wearing her enemy down on the dance floor while building a tight case against him for the day of reckoning or the Day of Judgment. For when the Woman is around, evil can't help itself but show up.

Satan is weak for the Woman, and he knows this. Satan is beneath the Woman and knows this as well. She is his greatest threat and always will be! No matter how hard the Devil tries, the Woman will always be his boss! She just needs to be sure that she's on the right side of God; because if she is not right, she will be left! God did not create the Woman to be Satan's assistant, but to be his boss! When Lucifer saw the Woman for the first time in Heaven, he could not keep his glory because the Woman's glory was too glorious! Her gift was personal, the gift of God's glory! She had so much glory until Lucifer started to transform into the Serpent, a dragon! This is why he was so mad, so furious with her.

What's funny is that she didn't even know him and still doesn't, while her very existence caused him to change. He couldn't keep his glory because she took it from him. She was clothed in glory, and now he is trying to clothe her in shame. He wants to clothe her in darkness when God clothed her with the sun, moon, and stars. Man, who can stand up to the Woman? We had better recognize the Woman! Women, be very careful that you don't be deceived into doing his dirty work and disqualifying yourself from going to Heaven where you really belong.

If you use your power to empower him, then you will be with him forever, just like the angels who he deceived, who were also cast down with him. They probably believed they could play both sides too, only to find out that there is a day when we all must give an account for the works that we do and have done.

If we take into account what happened in Heaven before the Woman and Serpent came to the earth, the Serpent had the upper hand. Eve was made and did not have a clue as to who she was. She did not know that the war between the Woman and Serpent had begun in eternity, not time. Here she finds herself in time and fighting a battle that is beyond her. She has to grow and mature, learning now what life is.

The Serpent talked to Eve, but he did not touch her. This shows how powerful words are. It demonstrates the impact our words have on any situation. This is why we must be careful about what we say and to whom we say it. It's not by chance that in this day and time, MCs and rappers hold the top of the charts. Words are our greatest influence. Everything that we know was created by words. Speakers, teachers, and preachers all use words, even God. When He walked in the Garden, He used His voice and words. The Serpent deceived the Woman with his voice and words. God told Adam that he is punished because he listened to his wife's voice and words. So if all this trouble started with words, then how can we not believe that words are alive?

Words move things. It's because of the power in our words that affect people every day. Words of all languages are moving the world right now. This is the power of the voice! The Woman was connected to the Serpent because of the words he had spoken to her. She heard the spoken word, and then she obeyed and listened. Then she used her words and voice to influence her husband to eat the forbidden fruit and disobey his God. He esteemed his wife over God Almighty. God created everything by His voice and words, so He knows the power of the spoken word. Now, can you see how the Woman was not mature and experienced enough to engage in deliberate deception? Adam was not deceived; he was in love! He knew what was going to happen to him, but he made a choice to be with his wife.

Maybe she ate the forbidden fruit because her husband was not there. Maybe he could have saved her if he had been with her to protect her. This happened while Adam was away at work. Sometimes our women are not covered or protected because we become too busy making money. We need balance. Adam knew what life would be like without Eve and did not want to go back to living that way again. Now that he'd experienced his wife, he did not want to live without her. He also understood that he did not protect her because he was too busy keeping and dressing the Garden but not having a balance with work and spending time with Eve led to his fall.

Satan saw his opportunity to get in-between them. If you read the Holy text, God gave the Woman a promise that she will be vindicated! God told Eve, "Your seed will bruise the seed of the serpent's head." The Woman's seed would be her warrior and deliverer! Amazingly, God did not say, "Adam's seed!" This is worth investigating. So why is there such a misinterpretation by men on this planet concerning the Woman? This war started against the Woman, and what kind of God or Father would have her to be silent or shut her mouth when her enemies are seeking to destroy and slandering her every day? What is this conspiracy! The Woman being silent is not the answer because she's not going to shut her mouth anyway! She speaks every chance she can get, even if behind closed doors. She has a need to express herself and to be heard by somebody. After the account in the Garden, we should recognize how powerful she is and help to cultivate her for greater use. Her voice damaged her family's place with God.

She caused them to lose their home, they were put out of paradise, and gave birth to jealousy and death. Her decision even affected her unborn children, causing her first-born son to kill his younger brother. Her husband now struggled to take care of them, never being able to catch up with bills. Until this happened, they had no bills, no debt. They were debt-free! This is the will of God for his children.

Now, after all of this history, the Woman is proven to be the most lethal weapon on this planet! Her voice is the voice heard in every language, every race, every creed, every nation, and in every organization; yes, it is the voice of the Woman that is heard in private. She has been the driving force for all generations, but she has remained "in the closet," and now it's time for her to come forth. We all are guilty of listening to her yet keeping her on the down-low. When she's not speaking with her mouth, she's talking with her body. She's the voice we respect in private and the body we show off in public. This puts a lot of pressure on her to look good because she knows she's being judged most of the time for her looks (outer appearance) and not her brains. She's the counselor, the voice we listen to anyway, but again, in private. Yes, we hear her through the media, even if she's not talking. We consider her in every move we make because she is the voice.

Her sons, yes, we hear her, through her husbands, yes, we hear her, through her brothers, oh yes, we hear her! The leaders in government and production houses everywhere listen to her before they release their products; even our music and the arts are built on her voice because her voice matters; yes, *we hear you*. Whether she's being lifted up or cast down, we hear her. And this hypocrisy needs to stop!

O, Woman! He needs your power, and in return, he'll give you power; oh, but the Woman is already powerful! Again, she just doesn't know it. When you don't understand this, you listen to your enemy, the Serpent, and use your God-given talents and power to give power to your enemy, the Satan.

Then he uses it against you to break up the home or your marriage, or start a war, or to get you to sell yourself for things rather than to save a life. Satan needs you! He is nothing without you! Listen to the voice inside you; is it the voice of good or evil? Are you building a life or tearing it down?

Look at what happens in the book of Genesis...

The Serpent deceives the Woman, but when approached by God, she doesn't lie. Do you know why? Because she is the truth. Every Woman was born good and pure, but the sinful nature of that Serpent is always after her.

If you don't have love or have experienced the true love of God, the ritual will fool you. Without love, it's all for nothing, and God is not in it! Going to a worship service does not make us righteous, Godly, or worthy of God's love.

IV

Chapter 4: The Serpent, The Woman, The Son

He is a liar, and the truth is not in him. He will get in the woman's mind if she doesn't resist and make her believe that his thoughts are her thoughts. He destroys her first by planting seeds of untruths in her mind. He is the master of painting pictures of imagination pulled from his previous life. He pushes his past pains onto her without her even knowing it. She must trust the voice of God within her, which is leading her away from this evil-doer. He is cunning and sly. He is poison; he is vicious and deadly.

"That girl is poison" when she allows the serpent to use her. He moves subtly and can be still and even comforting at times. He's patient at times, knowing just when to strike. He caresses you when you need to be comforted but will strike if he's not pleased with you. He is good at recognizing seasons. He knows how to lay low when it's cold and move on when it's hot. He selects his prey based upon fear, weakness, and inexperience. He knows your potential. He will squeeze the life out of you if given the chance. He will sacrifice you for a meal and the satisfaction that follows.

He will put his fangs in you and leave you, not even staying around to watch you die. When he strikes, it's so quick you don't see it coming. You just feel the effect of its venom. He knows when you're in need and how to fulfill that need. He knows the right things to say in the worst situations. He's kind and understanding, he's seductive.

He will give you babies of your own and some other babies too, from his affairs! He's not faithful to you but faithful to himself and his needs. He will always roll with his own kind and have you as one of his trophies. He is skilled in making you feel on top of the world, especially when you are at your lowest. He has a variety of approaches to be sure you don't figure him out, and if you do, he's done with you, at least for the time being. He's the Serpent.

He's the bad boy with charm, and somehow you are deceived by this to think you can contain him... it's a fantasy. He gets so much play by his experience that he will never be satisfied with just you. He hates you and keeps this undercover as long as you are in the dark. He tells his friends how much of a freak you are. He goes to great lengths, telling very private details about how you are in the bedroom. To you, it was intimate and personal, but to him, it was just another catch, a piece of tail! While you're in it with your feelings and emotions, he's there for the physical pleasures. He's emotionless, but how could you possibly know this as a young and inexperienced woman? You are looking for happiness, and he is too. The problem is, there are two totally different interpretations and perspectives on happiness. You're giving him milk and as-suming that he knows to buy the cow, but as long as he's get-ting the milk and doesn't have to buy the cow, he's cool. They used to say, "why buy the cow when you can get the milk for free?" The truth is, we today are willing to buy the milk, but not the cow.

So men always go, "What's the problem? When I took you out, took you shopping, or brought your kids something... I paid for that milk! When I made you reach an orgasm... I paid for that milk! When I'm ready for some more milk, I'll see you again. When you get stingy with the milk, I'll just start look-ing for another cow."

Women, you can't beat him at this game by being played this way. You were not designed for this kind of treatment.

I'm not coaching you to be vindictive and rebellious, but the opposite. Be real and what God created you to be—a queen. Use your power to be powerful, not destructive, be harmonious. This is what the world needs: unity and har-mony, wrapped together in love! You must use your intellect and your mind, not your body and your behind (butt)! Be a *head*, not somebody's *tail*! This is a vicious cycle in our world today. The woman must get her education, intellectually and spiritually!

Respect yourself and don't allow men or any other crea-ture to disrespect and discount your worth, or your greatness, given to you by God.

The woman's body is attached to a great heart until it has been broken. A broken heart will have echoes of broken rela-tionships if it does not take time to heal. But here comes the serpent again. He can sense when you're lonely and haven't had any in a long time. Instead of getting to know his heart, you get to know his head... the little one!

Well, how long do you think his little brain will be able to hang with you? While you are interpreting and equating good sex with a good relationship, he's already getting bored with you and looking at your girlfriend. A good relationship must have balance, and both parties must be on the same page.

The woman can have an affair emotionally and be very connected, while a man does not count it as such until he actually has sex with you. Just because a man has sex with you does not mean he's in a relationship with you. Note: sexually, there will always be another woman willing to do way more than you just did... the woman by nature is so creative and competitive that she can be her own enemy!

He is a master at playing this game, but to you, it is real life. After sex, you leave with all the expectations and more of what he said he was going to be to you (pillow talk). You think you are building a relationship, and he's using you until he finds the One? You know, *the One* who is worth the wait! Sometimes while he's with you, you may win him on a technicality because finding the One is taking longer than he had anticipated.

So some women get this type of man for the wrong reasons, and when he finds that girl, the One, he will hate you and mistreat you. He will turn on you and make you feel like nothing and blame it on your craziness. After this joker uses you, you are a prime candidate for abuse, a target for repeated failure and unhappiness. You will not trust any man or anyone and then push the real love out of your life. You will make him pay the price for the crap you've gone through with the dragon.

God intended for us to be in a committed relationship, but there's so much game out here, then I suggest that you date a man for 120 days without sex, *none*! During this time period, this is what's going to happen; you'll get to know his habits, his work ethic, his ways, some secrets (it's bound to happen), his friends, his true feelings about you, if he's available for you during the Holidays (this one is very important), how he handles pressure, whether his or yours or both. I could go on, but I hope you get the point?

You both need to know how this will play out or in, for that matter? For the first 40 days, the relationship is establishing law, the next 40 days is the prophetic or the proclamation for a future together, and the last 40 days is for what I call "the fulfillment of the two". If you make it through the 120 days, you guys will be so close, it will be impossible to stay apart; but he must be as transparent as you are.

You guys must become one; emotionally, spiritually, and physically... These 120 days are yours! For compatibility and long term, this is the test; either pass or fail, but do not cheat on the grade, because you will only be fooling yourself! If he's playing, this 120-day period will expose him like an "X-ray!" You'll see it all... you will feel like Super Woman!

Now when he's willing to wait for you, you can't recognize love because you are the product of lust! You've been lusted after all of your life, and love doesn't stand a chance because love never lived with you before. Most women talk to other hurt women, and this is no good because they will give lethal advice to one another. It's not intentional, of course, but nevertheless, the results are deadly!

The "assassins" of true love and happiness are the unresolved hurt and pain of past experiences. How many times have you said to your girl or friend, "girl, he is a dog!" When he's lied to you or used you for sex, you're thinking, "what a dog!"

The truth of the matter is this; the nature of what he did to you is not the nature of a dog. Thinking it's "the dog in him" is only a delusion and a diversion from the truth. It's not a true diagnosis. You're treating the wrong thing. You must first find out what the illness is in order to give proper treatment. As long you think he's a dog, you will treat him like a dog.

Think for a minute. You can train a dog. When you think you have trained a man, you are disappointed to find out he was training you! If that man is operating without a "righteous and moral conscience," it's not the dog in him but the serpent. The serpent is your enemy, not the dog.

That serpent is determined to destroy you. You are the worst thing to ever happen to him. How many times have you cried over a man and turned to your dog and started talking about him, "being a dog to you!"

If your dog could talk, he would say, "why are you talking about him being like a dog, but embracing me and loving on me? I am a dog, and we are not alike!" If you love a dog, feed a dog, take care of a dog, that dog will love you back. He will obey you, be there for you, go wherever you go, and for the most part, will be there when you leave and come back. So most unfaithful men are not dogs but serpents.

How many women have handled or raised poisonous

snakes? Not many, right? Therefore, how would you know its nature? Study or watch a Nature documentary, and you will see. You've been dealing with a snake!

The serpent is the father of the dragon and snake. If you study the serpent, he is the wisest of them all. He's been called "that old serpent, Satan and the Devil, the Deceiver!" He has so much experience!

So listen, women, your defense is, "be wise as serpents, but harmless as doves!" Don't become hard and callous but stay soft and sweet, for your real love because he's coming, and you've got to be ready, not bitter!

Just know this, the serpent is always trying to find his way in to destroy life, anything that is not like himself. You don't want him anyway! He doesn't come in for the kill right away, but after he has used you up for his purpose. He needs the woman for his master plan. His desire is to hurt her because he wishes he *were* her and that he was created like her. He is jealous of you and is always competing with you.

Remember the fairy-tails when the damsel would be in distress. She would be taken by the dragon and stored away in a tower, representing a place far away from family, friends, life, happiness, and love, away from her dreams... this place can also be "psychological!"

Your enemy strategically plans to get you to himself and, if possible, will destroy anyone who seeks to deliver you. This is why you need strong, courageous, and truthful, but not controlling, people in your life. The serpent did not make you, and he certainly does not love you; he's not even your type. He was sent to confuse you, to intimidate, and to make you an easy kill.

The dragon is wise enough to separate and isolate the damsel. Putting her in a place of safekeeping for him and his purpose. The dragon is obsessed with her and can't explain why. He hates her, so why even bother? Why have her? What's the point? We've got to know it's bigger than what we see, even for a fairy-tail? Have you noticed how she's on lockdown, but the dragon goes and comes as he pleases? Does this sound familiar?

The serpent's objective is to possess and own the woman. He wants to own her mind, her heart, her soul, her hopes and dreams, her gifts, her talents, her children, her worship, her purpose, and her destiny. She's everything he'll never be; therefore, he wants her as his property. This way, he gets to live his fantasy through her. This is why he's always trying to monitor her finances for his glory, not hers! She is his replacement!

Think about it, the serpent doesn't love, and neither can he. It's not his character or nature to do so. From the beginning, the serpent didn't touch the woman; he's never touched her. His power over her is simply by and through words. He is good with words, no matter the delivery. He has the gift and uses it to manipulate her. He needs the woman to believe him over God. He desperately seeks out the woman. He is a liar and makes a lie seem like the truth.

Don't believe the lie. If the serpent had the power and authority to destroy you, he would have gotten rid of you a long time ago. This suggests that the woman has something of great value to the serpent. She holds something priceless and irreplaceable. Her value is the kingdom to him. This is why he needs her. She possesses something he needs and can't find it anywhere else. The woman must know her value. He gets off on hurting her, causing her to fear, and hurting those who love the woman. Think for a minute, who loves the dragon? Nobody! He has made himself unlovable.

Damsel, keep looking out of that window because help is on the way. It will be somebody who is not afraid of the dragon. There are two things that the dragon is afraid of, and that are, "Water and fire!" Although he is a "Fire breathing dragon," fire is his enemy. Whoever comes to her rescue must have conquered both.

Lust imprisoned her, but love will save her and set her free. So never give up on love because love will never give up on you.

Don't allow the serpent to be the reason for you not loving again, because after he hurts and leaves you, he's gone to the next victim ... to him it's business! You're depressed, and he's gone on, don't give him this power over you! The serpent will have his day in court. He has deceived many. He's the spirit behind so many deaths and much pain. Many, small and great, have been victims of this snake.

Beware of false prophets who come in God's name. Beware of partners who have no respect for your God. They will certainly not have respect for you. What's the inspiration for the fairy-tale story in the first place? Where did it come from? Everything we see comes from something we cannot see. Everything that is manifested has an origin. What we see is the fruit of some tree. So, why is this dragon guarding the tower where he's placed the woman? Why is she there? Why a tower? Why is she placed where only the dragon can get to her? Who will fight for her?

He would not be on guard if there were no hope of her being delivered or rescued. So no matter what you go through or have gone through and maybe are still going through, your enemy knows that there is a way out for you. You need to know this and never give up hope of being rescued. From the beginning, it has been a war between the woman and the serpent, in eternity and time. From the universe to the earth, from the Heavens to the Garden, her existence is always interrupted by the jealousy, fury, and hate of the serpent.

I hope you understand by now, when I say, "Serpent" I am not speaking of the physical but the spiritual manifestation through bodied vessels. When anyone has lied about you, hated you, or been jealous of you, had wicked intentions, been abusive toward you, or always tried to tear down whatever you do, told you nothing is good enough, found faults in you, and criticized your works and efforts, even if they are good, it is the work of your enemy, "the Serpent".

Stop looking at the race, gender, title, and position, etc. If someone is evil and has evil intentions toward you, it is the serpent! The serpent has a trinity as well. It's "The serpent, the dragon, and the snake." Study these characteristics without being judgmental and paranoid. You will be surprised by what you can see. See through the eyes of the "One" who created you and not through the blinding eyes of your enemies. "If the blind, lead the blind, then you both will fall in a ditch!"

I hope to see you get out of that ditch with the healing of your blinded eyes so you can see a whole new world with endless possibilities...

You are not what they say you are, so don't entertain them. After a while, they will move on, at least for a period, until the evil in them revises a plan, then they will try again. You are the star of the story, so get used to it! The serpent can't make it without you! He's always talking about you, trying to find fault in you. He is your greatest critic! He is your number one hater, and he's so sick, he's your number one fan as well, as long as you're on top of the charts!

These people are vessels for the serpent; they abide by his will! You must abide by your Father's Will, even more so! Keep doing good and let them talk. That's all they are... vessels who talk. Be mindful of this; the serpent is after you, your seed (children and even your unborn children). He knows the woman is God's greatest expression of created love and is a more valuable asset, so for that reason, he hates the woman. He pretends to like her, but this is a ploy to stay close to her in order to know her business. He needs something to work with; he does not like guessing. So stop telling him your business!

Make him work hard for whatever he gets from you, even information! This account of the serpent and the woman is in eternity. This place is before the account of his being cast down into time or the earth with Adam and Eve. The relationship between the woman and the serpent started long before the serpent and Eve in the Garden of Eden. Their fight began in eternity, long before time. Time is a module, taken out of eternity, not the other way around.

Anything we see in this world is the fruit of something from eternity unrevealed. Satan, being cast down from Heaven, is no different than the uprooting of a tree you no longer want in your garden. If it is producing something bad or unprofitable, get rid of it!

Well, Lucifer became unprofitable and was a threat to the good of Heaven, so he was up-rooted and exposed for who he really was; whether that may be a spirit, a thought, intent of hidden things of the heart, or a plot. Time is the place where all of this is manifested or brought to life. We may think we are smart and crafty, but the reality is this; all things hidden in eternity are now all things exposed through time, through every generation!

Likewise, the serpent again didn't show up until the woman showed her place when it came to the Son of God. This was when the enemy tried to kill her seed. As the child grew up, he posed no threat to royalty, wealth, and prosperity, and the kings of the earth went on as if nothing had happened; in other words, there were no reports of a new king or kingdom in the land. While they were looking for a natural king with king things, God had disguised Himself (Son) in poverty and humility!

His Majesty grew up as the son of a poor carpenter... surely this is no threat. Mary and Joseph must be thinking, "Maybe we all misinterpreted what God was saying to us." God came in humility to draw those who truly love and belong to Him, not the gold-digging religious folks who are in it for the money and not the love of God and His people.

The Woman must be careful how she deals with disappointment and pain because sometimes the serpent will use the mother to fight against her son because the enemy knows the son can see him for who and what he is and will ultimately destroy him!

God separated good from evil before it could manifest. If all of this evil that we are experiencing on earth through time had been released in Heaven, it would have been a mess. These things would have taken place in God's home, and the King would not have it! God's infinite wisdom got it out of Heaven, which would have been an eternal war, by sending it to time. It has been divided into many battles throughout many nations, races, generations, and times. In time, all things will be settled forever! Every life situation is a link to some heavenly account purposed by God or perpetrated by the Devil. Lucifer was a double agent, traitor, backstabber, liar, adulterer, murderer, thief, and player who got played! He thought he was outsmarting God, but this is impossible, and his children think they are doing the same on earth. They somehow see patience and mercy as weaknesses. God gave Lucifer and his angels space to come clean, so it could be fixed, and this fool interpreted it as God being slow or not having a clue as to what he was doing.

I'll go into more details throughout the book. Whenever you feel good about tearing someone down to destroy them, you are not working for God and His kingdom... it doesn't matter the position, title, or religion. You only tear down for the purposes of rebuilding again and not with innocent blood on your hands. Holiness is not going to church or what you say or how you dress, but it is a trait. Holiness is purity, love, joy, and goodness.

It is the very essence of peace without interruption or fear. God is love, joy, purity, and goodness by nature, and it's not an act. You can't *act* holy. That's ridiculous to even think such a thing. When Jesus was crucified, it was the high priest, priests, and religious leaders of Israel who lied and manipulated the Law of Moses to have Jesus put to death. The men were anointed priests and they abused their authority and power. The Pharisees represented Lucifer while the Romans represented Satan... see the partnership and unity to get the job done? Lucifer, through the religious leaders, manipulated the execution while not getting his hands dirty and Satan, through the Romans, carried out the order, by doing the dirty work.

This is the story of the Serpent, the Woman, and the Son...

The serpent is after her so badly that he sends a flood out of his mouth in hopes of carrying her away. "But the earth helps the woman and opens up its mouth to swallow the flood." The serpent is after her mind; this is what the flood represents, the woman is made in stereo, and the serpent is mono. He hates her more and feels the need to get rid of her. For 1260 days, this takes place, and the serpent is not giving up!

Yeshua represents this son, and his mother is unable to support his ministry for this 3-1/2-year period. Satan is after her mind. This is established in the Heavens before time. The war between them is a harsh reality. Mary went through her tribulation period while her Son was doing His Father's work.

V

Chapter 5: Serpent's Production

The serpent's employees; their job is to get her audience hyped up enough to believe they are really *gonna get* something. Each dance becomes more intense with seduction, taking her victims on a journey of lust. It can become so intense that some men lose control and put their hands on her because they feel they just *gotta* have her. Lust takes them over! The reality is, they get hooked on the fantasy! People keep coming back because it felt so good and close the last time that they think, "maybe I can get it this time." See, that's the fantasy! She's skilled to wrap and crawl that pole like a snake, slithering her way down to the stage in the most seductive way, releasing that serpentine fire!

The serpent uses sex to make her a "sex goddess". In this atmosphere, the club becomes the temple, the dancer becomes a god, and the stage is the altar. This is a modern depiction of ancient ritualistic worship. Don't underestimate the power of worship. Sex is used as a gateway to worship. Worship is not a religious act but the power to totally surrender to something or someone (honoring, paying homage, adoring) for the use of service to please or be pleased, without reserve or regard. Worship originated in heaven; it was and still is honorable for everyday life.

It's not just a religious act but an expression of love and servitude. We were born to worship, created to serve. It was the relationship that brought on the worship, not a law. When a woman becomes one with this serpent, he takes her over in mind, and she transmits through her body what message he wants to send to her victims; uncontrollable lust, transmitted through the eyes. If successful, then they feel they *gotta* have it! It's a trade, "the love of money for the lust of honey!" Both are traps in which neither can be fulfilled or satisfied!

He makes anyone who submits to him (through her) give him the money. The money is now laid at the altar, and this is where the sacrifice begins. This spirit is now in control and requires all who are there to participate in the worship, or makes one feel awkward or left out. Some even have been escorted out of the club for not participating. While under this spell, the serpent will ask you for your money, all money, no matter what it's for.

"Go to the ATM and get some more." It does not care about your life or situation. He is a destroyer of trust, families, and marriages at all costs. We are no challenge for him without Godly wisdom. Some guys would fight and break away to go outside of the temple (club) just to try and shake off the spell. Most people don't even know what quite happened to them. They feel dizzy after the fact because they found that they "overspent" on something that was "under-delivered!" Many are married and in committed relationships and have to go home feeling like a drug addict who spent the bill money on a lie! This is another lie by Satan to destroy the good. The ritual is wrapped in a beautiful package (naked-ness) to cause their victims to be overtaken with unfulfilled lust, and we know, where ever lust is, you will find corrup-tion. Lust will find a way!

This viper has bitten people from all walks of life. He's deadly! Many in this worship process have become liars and deceivers. Their wives and families don't even know them anymore. The reason for this is that they have been possessed by demonic spirits, which came in by way of worship in the clubs. It is a spirit that comes with everything forbidden. There's a price to pay when you play on the Devil's play-ground. It all starts out as fun, but the end is a horror story. Many people make it out, but few tell their stories, leaving the next victims defenseless against this poison called "fun!" Many divorces and break-ups have been caused by this "Devil's Den" or "Snake Pit!" Sadly, many have never told their loved ones about the real cause of their change of behavior because of the shame and embarrassment that would follow. Pride will allow them to act as though they don't care. This viper has even bit-ten celebrities. He will take their money too, to no end, and make them feel as though they are on top of the world until they cannot pay their bills. They are poisoned, and "another one bites the dust." They lose everything and have nothing to show for this worshiping. This is why Satan is called a thief, a deceiver, and a liar... That old serpent, he's been around since the ancient days. The serpent is in the business of exchange, especially unfair exchange: pleasure for pain, good times for bad times, life for death, he's always bargaining, and we have no clue without God as to what we have bargained for. Satan is very territorial; he has regions working his plan. This is the reason why certain areas are known for specific things. We travel to certain places with the confidence of getting or obtaining something we wouldn't, under normal circumstances acquire or achieve. Satan rules "principalities and powers, spiritual wickedness; in high places." This means he knows kingdom protocol and order. He was a prince, and his vengeance stems from long ago, a war in Heaven that he lost, and he's still sore about it. This is the drive behind his hate. He misses ruling the most powerful dominion ever...God's throne; the throne of "The Most High God!"

Recognize your adversaries; they will follow you to keep up with your life, only to find fault. If you have such a problem with me, then why bother? They're always finding fault in you or something wrong with what you do, but in reality, they cannot fill your shoes. They live their life through you because they are not satisfied with their own lives, but they would never admit it. Most critics could not live your life even for a week, and you have it for a lifetime! Most could not stand up to your daily pressures. Well, this is their daddy; this is his spirit, the spirit of the "condemner and critic!" Most critics who have so much to say about you couldn't carry 10 percent of the weight you carry. Most of them do not have your talents and gifts but always have something negative to say about you. They are all mouth and live to be you. "Jealousy is crueler than the grave!" We live in a "fickle" world, and it is not constant or loyal to anyone.

Look at our history. We have had some of the greatest people ever to walk this planet in our own generation, and still, we have mistreated them when they needed us the most. We have used their gifts and talents to see us through some of the toughest times. They have helped us celebrate some of our most memorable moments with our loved ones, from weddings to funerals, graduations, family reunions, church, and even more. We have had some of the greatest memories because of the sacrifices and gifts these persons have given and made for us. But when they made a mistake or were going through their own challenges, we cruelly, with no mercy, threw them under the bus and left them for dead. Yes, we have let them down. It takes having a pure heart to be loyal. So I would encourage any woman who has made great achievements to be thankful to God, who is the giver of her talents and gifts. Be loyal to Him, for He'll always be there for you. Your talents and gifts are your stamps of endorsement by God to do what you've done. Be sure to be ready to meet your true Father when your time is finished here. He will never change toward you, no matter what.

Sometimes we need to be sensitive to the times and seasons we are in and not allow the enemy to torment us into believing we need to compete with our own achievements and prove ourselves all over again. Free yourself and your mind from other people's expectations and enjoy the blessings God has given you. Find something or someone new who will appreciate and love you for the true gift that you are. There is another you deep down on the inside; let the old you go and make room for the new you...be encouraged, be grateful, happy, and joyful. God is there when you're young and beautiful, and He's there when you're old and wrinkly. Through His eyes, you will always be young and beautiful. When you go to your eternal home, He will have a new glorious body for you that will never age or lose its radiant beauty! He'll never change His feelings about you, whether you're popular or not so popular because He's your loving Father and will always be there to see you through. When the world throws you away for another, God is always right there. Just talk to Him, and if you just listen, He will remind you about who you are and *whose* you are.

When you finish your journey here, just come on home to the place where your real family and friends are. Your kingdom family will never change on you, but love you unconditionally with celebration! Trust and believe, those who have gone on before us, who are God's children, would never want to come back here. They remember the fight, just trying to do good and helping to make the world a better place. One lifetime here is enough to fight evil. They used their God-given talents for that purpose, and sure, God blessed them with a good life, but they had so many haters. This is what makes us like Him; "And He was hated without a cause!" But now that they are gone, they are in eternal bliss! Stay with God, and you will never lose. "Weeping endures for a night!" So no matter how much pain you go through, it's equivalent to only one night.

Study your enemy, and don't allow him to make a fool out of you. Know this; one out of one who is born, will die and after death, we will give an account of whose kingdom we worked for while on this planet. Everyone who lived here before us, from the greatest to the smallest person, wishes they could come back to tell us, "It's not worth it if you're working for God's enemy. Everything belongs to God anyway, and Satan is bargaining with riches and wealth that does not belong to him anyway. No one takes anything with them from this earth, and not even Satan can take a thing from here to the underworld. He must decorate his kingdom below with his own stuff. You will find this little factoid about him; he's not creative; he's only good at stealing the good, which God created. If there's any good in him, then he's good at recognizing what's good, not creating it! Because when it's all said and done, when we take our last breath in time, we will take our first breath in eternity, and the worst thing that can ever happen to us is not in time but eternity.

We can afford to lose things in time, but we don't want to suffer losses in eternity; we need to fix it now, while we have a chance. He sends weapons to destroy lives, relationships, and marriages. This is spiritual. What else could it be? Like anything else, there are exceptions; somebody will always cross the line. So now and again, you might get some. In this compact, the woman feels very powerful! She feels like somebody is listening to her, even if it's only her body language. Somebody gave her a voice, and somebody's listening. So, will God judge her more than the preacher who sells the fantasy? Now she is educated, she is experienced, she is strong, she is courageous, she is tired, but she is not weak! She must be heard as the voice called by Almighty God! We are not talking about rebellion against righteousness but a trumpet for change, for life!

She must fulfill her destiny and get revenge for her losses. We have used her body for many things, but now it's time to use her voice! It's time to listen to her, not just listen, but *hear* her and take her seriously. She has paid a hefty price to be heard. She used her voice against God's order, and now, to make it right, she must, in return, use her voice to set things back in order! We must give her this. The woman and the serpent united to bring this mess, so now the woman must destroy the serpent and unite with her man to re-establish order! Wake up people. The writing is on the wall. She can build the church by frying chicken and fish, but men are too insecure to support them and give them the voice to restore the family that she destroyed by default!

Whether we like it or not, God is a God of order, and the woman's repentance for the garden is restitution by her using her voice to build and obey the Will of Almighty God. A woman will rule in the Free World as the superpower and voice in this New Millennium! Because of the serpent's hate for her and how he's stolen from her, and how he's been after her mind...oh yes, he wants her mind! God will make you president of the United States of America. Only the woman can make this right! It all fell apart from the very beginning, a war between the woman and the serpent. She will avenge herself and those who the serpent hates. Women must unite for the greater good, which is desperately needed in the world today. The woman will win this time! She has learned and is very seasoned and experienced; now she is ready, working with a purpose. She's not naive or blind anymore, and she has a vision. Her vision is God's vision, and it will come to pass. It's the prophecy! God will bless her with His glory just as He did in the Heavens (Eternity) before (Time) the earth! He's looking for the one who will now listen to His voice so that He may become her voice! She must pray and know God's voice! He's not interested in a religious woman but a woman who knows Him because she is in a relationship with Him. What does this mean? It is simple; she knows His voice and will stand on that and will no longer do what the serpentine voice is telling her! She will set up all things as planned by God for this last season. We cannot have Armageddon without her. The Anti-Christ will not get his position without her. Just as the heart of Lucifer was revealed through the hate he had for the woman, so shall it be when the woman takes her position as president. This will cause him to come out of hiding. This will cause him to compete with her, and she will rule well and with Godly wisdom, bringing much-needed changes to government as a whole. Policies that seemed impossible will supernaturally turn around. She will get the support because God has ordained heaven and earth to cooperate and work with her. The leaders to this point were anointed, but the woman, chosen and ordained by God will be anointed and wrapped with glory! The glory of God is the missing ingredient as the woman is the only one who was created in God's glory.

We as men have been privileged to see the glory, but the woman was created in it. Only one man could handle and was given the glory, and that was more than 2,000 years ago! The last time the glory was here time started over to what we call, "B.C. and A.D." Oh yes, that was the glory! Why else would time start over in honor of a poor carpenter? Now come on, folks, this doesn't make any kind of sense, except it's *gotta* be the glory! The whole world should have fought against time, starting over to his honor. Who is this poor man anyway? I think we all know the answer! The world can't agree on much, but when the glory is present, things begin to move! Well, get ready, because it's about to move! The world is in need of a real miracle, and miracles only happen when God's glory is present! We are about to witness a shift in the whole world! This woman must understand how treacherous Jezebel was and be the opposite! Learn about your enemy, the serpent, and avenge yourself by not listening to him, but listen to your heavenly Father, who is God! "We pray for your strength in the Lord! God bless you, and God Bless America."

The Devil is skilled in making you feel on top of the world when you are at your lowest. He has a variety of approaches to be sure you don't figure him out, and if you do, he's done with you by now anyway. He's the serpent. He's the bad boy with charm, and somehow, you are deceived by this to think you can contain him...it's a fantasy. He gets so much play by his experience that he will never be satisfied with just you.

The serpent did not make you and certainly doesn't love you; he's not even your type. He was sent to confuse you.

God made you, He loves you, and He is Holy. But holiness is not a religion or some *Why I Hate the Woman* religious act.

Holiness is not going to Church or Mosque, partaking in a religious service, nor is it what you say or how you dress, but it is a nature. Holiness is purity, life, love, kindness, compassion, and goodness. It is the very essence of peace without interruption or fear. God is love, purity, and goodness by nature and it's not an act. God is love and no matter what our gifts are and how powerful we may be, if you don't have love, you have nothing! You can't act holy. It's ridiculous to even think such a thing. Holiness is DNA, and if you are Holy, it's because God is in you; there's no other reason! It's the reason why some will never change or turnaround from wicked deeds; they carry the DNA of their father...the Devil.

We try to reason with them all day every day, but they are blind to the truth, even when it's right there plainly in their faces. They will never apologize or repent for the evil they have done. They will not turn from their wicked ways because they are evil and do what pleases their father, the Devil. Satan does not repent for anything; it's not his nature to do so. This is how you will know who he is and who his children are...

VI

Chapter 6: Created on Purpose

She is the greatest of all God's creations!

It is said that when God created man in His own image, He created him in pairs; male and female. This implies that both characters and natures of male and female were already in the first man. Adam in creation was already supplied with his companion, which means that procreation was always within him. When the time came, God put Adam to sleep, took out one of his ribs, and made the woman! It's interesting to know that the woman at the beginning of creation came out of the man. When Adam recovered from this procedure, he saw the being for the first time and called her "woman" because she was taken out *of* the *man*. She was *of man*.

She was the first and only thing that looked like himself but was distinguished from him by some obvious, notably extras that made her female. This was the evidence that she had been given some things that man did not possess...seen and unseen, for obvious reasons, which will later be discovered. Adam was so pleased with the gift that God had given him, and God called her "Adam's helper or help-meet." This meant the woman was supposed to help him fulfill his purpose and destiny. In the beginning, we must understand, God created and prepared everything first for Adam to have in place before the woman was even brought forth. This is why it's the very nature of a woman to desire security and nice or good things in life. When having that threatened or seems difficult to achieve, she goes into the *"I must make this happen by any means"* mode, especially if she has children. From the very beginning, this was not so, it was not the woman's responsibility to take care of the household and or family alone or as a sole provider... in fact, this is a curse.

When God created man, He created him in His own image and with His nature. Adam was God's son, which made Adam the prince and God, the King of the universe! So Adam was the prince, having dominion or all authority in this world. Everything listened to Adam. There were no divisions or rebellions of nature. It's important to understand where Adam came from in order to even begin to understand the woman. Everything that was created by God was given the power to reproduce after its own kind. Everything was subjected to this law of procreation. The greatest reward in all life is the fulfillment of being the best at what we were created to be. Life was beautiful...no stresses, no opposition, no chaos. For example: what if the sun was jealous of the moon or the stars, the planets, or what if the fish wanted to be birds, and birds wanted to be reptiles? Think about the animals wanting to be humans, or going to an apple tree, which had apples with part of an orange growing on the inside and saying, *"I always felt like I should have been an orange."* Imagine how chaotic the universe and worlds would be if the creations rebelled against their true and natural origins, causing the power and purpose of reproducing to be annihilated. What if everything God created decided to rebel and just did its own thing? Do we really not understand that had God not intervened, we would not have existed?

What is famine? Suppose the earth decided not to bring forth any crops, or the birds protested and would not produce or mate. Consider what would happen if the fish of the sea have a meeting and call for a strike; no more seafood for the humans? Or what if everything just started hating? Hating its species, its origin, its way of life, even the one who created them out of sheer rebellion? Look at the things that we really don't have any control over, such as the sun rising and the moonlight shining in the night sky; or the world turning and the existence of both saltwater and freshwater. What if everything created with a purpose decided they didn't want to be what they were created to be? How long would life, as we know it, last? So, we need to have some respect for the brilliant mind that created purpose and all things...we need love! Love gives, but hate takes!

How would we survive? It's a numbers game; see, we take for granted that the evil and hate that steals, takes, and destroys will be supplemented but by what? Do we depend on the natural or corrective way of creation to fix it? How selfish of, whatever that spirit is, that uses *us* against *us*! What ignorance and selfishness! There were no divisions, chaos, or wars; just peace and harmony...the lion laid down with the lamb.

When man was created, God also gave him instructions before the woman even came on the scene. Man had responsibilities given directly from God. There was no sweat or hard labor but just the upkeep (maintenance).

Imagine no rent, no mortgage, no utility bills, no taxes, no car payments, no grocery bills, no need for credit card debt, no insurance, no need for any of these things. God had provided for every need in creation. When He created everything, He did it with Adam in mind. Just as a parent would prepare a nursery for an unborn, expected child. Everything was for Adam to enjoy, everything that is, except one tree. Without this tree, man would be robbed of his power to choose. God gave us the free will to choose. We must choose good or evil. We will never accuse God of having a choice. Out of all His creation and beauty, it's only one thing he cannot have, the tree of knowledge, good and evil. This defies religious folks, who are afraid to live because they think everything is a sin. If Adam had everything to choose from except one tree, and he still messed up, then what in the world are we supposed to do when religious folks make everything a sin?

This is why we have so many hypocrites wearing masks every day before COVID-19 because they cannot live up to the tall order themselves. Therefore they hide to have a good time...God is not cruel or goofy like that! I think they will judge Jesus when they see Him if they see Him in heaven when He drinks a glass of wine. They would probably call Him a devil again. He already told His disciples that He would drink new wine with them in the Kingdom. Not being in harmony with the Creator to fulfill your purpose will bring about worries, stress, anxiety, frustrations, fears, and insecurities. This is not about religion but the eternal Kingdom, the Kingdom that is an eternal establishment or government.

No matter who you are, understand this, you belong to one of two kingdoms, the Kingdom of Love and Life or the Kingdom of Hate and Death. One is ruled with love and delivering life and needs, while the other is self-centered, fueled by lust, hate, and greed. The weak, no matter how great, will acknowledge a greater source than themselves as the reason for their success and achievements and turn to Him in times of challenge or failure.

The wicked ones, however, will always seek to take over something that's not theirs in the first place. They are never content, no matter how much they have or how much power they possess. They live as though they will never die. They never admit to doing wrong or turn from their evil to save a life but selfishly continue at all costs to achieve their goals without regard for another life. Born of the flesh, we are either weak or wicked! We are born on purpose with an expiration date. In time, we will expose who we *really* are and *whose* we are. Be wise and careful not to partner with your greatest enemy to destroy you and your family.

Eve did not understand that she was sold a lie. It was very intriguing for pleasure but with very lethal results. The Serpent was positioned on the tree that God told them not to eat from. While he was talking to the woman, he knew she would not be able to resist if she continued to listen to him... Don't listen, but resist, and he will flee. Adam was innocent with no worldly experience; so can you imagine the difference in the Serpent's words with all of his experience? Eve had never heard such wisdom, what subtle enticement. Everything has a purpose, good or evil, and even the Serpent was created on purpose...

VII

Chapter 7: The Deception

Genesis is the book of beginnings for the world's creations and life here on earth but Revelation is the book of the account of eternity before time.

Time is a module taken out of eternity for the purpose of fulfillment, purpose, exposure, and judgment. So simply put, Revelation is before Genesis. What's in Revelation happened first! This is very interesting. Get this and you will never be the same again! The 12th chapter of Revelation is an account of eternity and the third chapter of Genesis is tied together. Revelation is an account of the past, present, and future. Most times when you hear the story of Adam and Eve, you hear about how Eve ate of the fruit and gave it to her husband. I would like to go a little deeper. The Bible speaks about the Lamb slain before the foundation of the world. This means that the answer for man's mistakes or sins was already in place. The solution was there before the problem.

When the Son was caught up to His God he was prepared for the sacrifice. It was already written in heaven that humanity would fall short. God already had Adam and Eve's back, so it was Satan who got played; he just didn't know it at the time. God told Adam he could freely eat of every tree in the garden but to not eat of the tree of the knowledge of good and evil. This defies religion and the suggestion about God not wanting us to enjoy life. Of all God's creations, He created everything for Adam and Eve's pleasure and enjoyment, just as good parents prepare a place for their unborn child, such as painting and furnishing a nursery. Everything is prepared for that child. God prepared everything for them in advance for their pleasure. It was one tree, and one tree only, out of the garden that they were told stay away from and were commanded not to eat from its fruit. If you're like me, you might say, why put the tree there in the first place? Maybe this trouble could have been avoided.

God's infinite wisdom is starting over with His own life and we are in the plan. God is now building His own family and that is why man was created in God's image and His likeness. Adam and Eve are the first beings to be like God Himself. This had to be a site for the angels and heaven. Lucifer was thrown down out of heaven with some stuff hidden in his heart and this is the place where it all will be revealed! But how? God knew Lucifer was up to no good while in charge in heaven and though he did some bad and contrary things, most of them were secrets of the heart. Iniquity was hidden in his heart; this is compared to a woman being full-term pregnant and in labor ready to deliver. Temptation induces the labor for that evil to come out of him. It was a setup, because Lucifer would never admit his hate for God and intent to takeover heaven, especially the plot to kill God. He would

have made an example of God to put fear into the other angels so they would never ever think about doing to him what
he wanted to do to God. This was a brutal plan! But God
could see and know his heart. On purpose, God's timing in
casting Lucifer down and his angels was for them to see their
replacement—the new creation and masterpiece; the Woman!
He transformed to a serpent/dragon while almost hypnoti-
cally gazing at the awesome beauty and glory of this great
wonder... the Woman!

Now that Lucifer was in the earth as a serpent, although
Adam was in the garden, the serpent didn't even make his
presence known. He did not show himself until Eve showed
up. When Adam praised her beauty as the heavens did the
woman in eternity, it was then the serpent went to work. Notice how the serpent was not even mentioned until Eve came
into existence; she was his focus and target. She is what he saw
in heaven, not Adam. It was the woman giving life from her
body and this devil will never forget that! He tried to destroy
her there while in eternity but could not, because she received
help and got away! He hates the Woman! He feels she is the
reason for him being thrown out of heaven. He's in denial, like
most are when they are full of pride and will not turn from
wrongdoing to make a change. He is so wicked, that he is not
taking responsibility for what he's done. He has deceived himself to believe that God does not know how evil he is. Why?
Because it's hidden in his heart! God has set him up and he
didn't even know it! All the evil in his heart must come out to
be dealt with and eliminated forever.

We need the woman to make this happen. He is so blinded
with hate for her that he goes in on her right away to have a

talk to see where her head is. While the serpent is talking to her, he is practicing the same hypocrisy he was committing in heaven, grinning in the face of God and the holy angels. His heart is full of evil. He doesn't know it yet, but God can see what's in his heart. God's goal is to get what's in his heart to come out of hiding. Guess who was hired for the job? That's right, the Woman! Have you ever thought, why didn't the serpent talk to Adam? Reason being, it was the woman that he saw in eternity. She was his replacement, his greatest enemy, but she was innocent. The serpent started to go in on her and he asked Eve, "Did God say you cannot eat of all the trees in the garden?"

She said, "Yes, we can eat of all the trees except the tree in the midst of the garden. Do not eat of it, for in the day that you eat, you will surely die."

The serpent said to the woman, "That's not what God said, for He knows in the day that you eat, you will become like gods."

The serpent put a twist on the truth and convinced Eve to disobey God. Lucifer knew that this would get her out of God's favor. He needed her to be on the outs with God. See how low down and dirty he was. This is his same practice to this day. He is a liar and a deceiver. Adam is in a grown man's body but Adam is innocent as well. Adam and Eve are really equivalent to minors; they have no experience at all. They are so brand new to life. They are naked and don't even know it at this point. They have not been introduced to sex at the time of the serpent's approach to them. This is a real misconception to think they have had any interactions intimately. This is why the serpent is so effective. The serpent preyed on their inexperience of life. He moved like a pimp and hustler taking advantage of a runaway teen.

Eve was curious and his approach was very gentle, appearing helpful and intriguing. Imagining what Adam's conversation was like compared to the serpent's was that Adam is on Eve's level, maybe just a little more, while the serpent has and is speaking with experience from throughout eternity! Eve didn't stand a chance, but God already knew this; however, Lucifer's heart must be exposed and all creation is to witness this and to go on record because the angels don't know how corrupted Lucifer is as of yet. The serpent was in rear form, feeling the power of becoming one with Satan; he had given himself over to be used. He was so wise to talk to Eve from the tree that she was not supposed to eat from in a cunning way. He was in the right place and position, while Eve was in the wrong place. That's why a woman must be watchful if she is vulnerable, to not be in a place of lions, dogs, or wolves when she is a lamb. Now the serpent knows it's only a matter of time before the woman eats and he can make his next move. He knows that if he can get her he can get her husband, her unborn children, her family, her purpose and her destiny—all in hopes of getting to her God!

This enemy desires of all things to make God hurt. He wants to burn God so bad that he can taste it! Eve finally eats the forbidden fruit and her eyes open! What does this mean? She sees the fruit as good to eat and pleasurable for food. Her innocence is gone. She's gone from the mind of a child to a full-blown experienced woman of the world. She can see visions of all kinds of things to do with her body and Adam's. Satan is showing her visions of how to work her body and seduce Adam and by doing so, gain control of him. This is the introduction of witchcraft! All this time, they may as well have been five years old before they ate of the forbidden tree. Sexuality is a gift from God and was never intended to be used for our destruction. It was a gift you couldn't get from the store, but only from God and it was the gift given for a committed relationship. God invested too much time and thought before engineering such a thing; it was designed to enhance the experience not diminish it! Eve was aroused. She has never felt this way before, and she could not help but think the serpent was powerful. She called her husband to get him to eat. Now Adam was like most responsible men; he was a workaholic and didn't even know it. He was working before Eve came and was excited to meet her and have her, but he got caught up in his job. When God first instructed Adam of his duties and responsibilities, he told him to keep and dress the garden, which means taking care of it and keeping it neat and clean. He also gave him the responsibility of naming all the animals, birds, and so forth. Adam had a job and liked his job. Adam was dedicated and faithful to his job. Every day God would visit with them. Adam was like a child running to greet his father or mother coming in from work. The serpent was saying to Eve, "Do you want Adam to notice you like that? Do you want him to worship you and be just as excited? Well, I can show you how. Just eat where I eat, from this tree." Man, that serpent was working on her. Have you ever had someone that you never thought you would give them the time of day, but they just wouldn't quit and take "no" for an answer. Well, this is Satan at his best... he is consistent!

In the meantime, Adam forgot one important detail... his

wife. She was at the tree while Adam was at work. So many affairs have happened this way. This idle time is dangerous. Adam was supposed to love, protect, and cover his wife at all costs. He was a little caught up with his life. Maybe he was also a little too secure in his relationship and as long as another man was not around, he did not pose any other species as a threat! Watch out men; learn from Adam! Many men today have lost their wives to a lie, a religion, a cause, a job, money, a credit card, shopping, a salon, a woman, a boy-toy, a toy, a drug, a pet, a device, a club, a pole, a player, a pimp, a hustler, a "Battery-Operated-Boyfriend", and even the television! As a result, some attempt suicide, others suffer from depression or have mental illnesses. Many make attempts but are given a second chance. We don't know how notorious the battle of the mind can be when it turns into war and you're trying to figure out how you got here and what war this is. You know you did not sign up for this but nonetheless, you must fight or lose everything! I need somebody, anybody to tell me the truth! The devil cannot speak the truth because he's a liar!

The serpent has many ways to get to the woman! His ultimate goal is to destroy her and her dreams, her marriage, her family, her joy, her peace, her every chance to be happy, by any means necessary. Eve then gives to her husband to eat and he takes it freely. Now Adam's eyes were opened! He was being educated and seduced by the wily snake. Adam knew nothing but the things of God while Eve was getting the low down in the streets. Eve now knew what her body could do and was aroused and stimulated despite not being touched! The serpent did not touch her but drew her in by his talk! That fruit was like a drug... she had to have it. When Eve influenced Adam, everything changed because a woman can be very persuasive. When God made her, he equipped her with power and glory! Nothing is greater than a Wife and a Mother! Look throughout history and credit them! The woman in eternity proves that! She was married, had a child and started a war just with her presence. She didn't say a word—just showed up! Nothing is greater than a woman that knows who she is and submits to her God, is powerful but humble, gives advice and receives instruction, but can recognize foolishness and shuns it with class and grace. She knows how to move on and stay focused to save others while securing the future. A good woman is priceless! Now, after Eve ate and gave to her husband, God visited Adam. They heard the Voice of the Lord God walking in the garden and Adam took Eve and hid from the presence of God for the first time ever.

He was also afraid for the first time. He does not know or understand these emotions but is reacting to them. They hid among the fig trees and covered themselves with fig leaves. God called out and said, "Adam where are you?"

And he said, "I heard your voice and I was afraid, because I was naked; and I hid myself."

And God said, "Who told you that you were naked? Have you eaten from the tree that I commanded you not to eat from?"

Then the man said, "The woman whom you gave to be with me, she gave me of the tree, and I did eat."

The Lord God said to the woman, "What is this that you have done?"

And the woman said, "The serpent deceived me, and I did eat."

And the Lord God said to the serpent, "Because you have done this, You are cursed above all cattle, and every beast of the field: on your belly you will go, and dust you will eat all the days of your life: And I will put enmity (the state or feeling of being actively opposed or hostile to someone or something) between you and the woman, and between your seed and her seed; her seed will bruise your head and your seed will bruise her seed's heel."

To the woman God said, "I will greatly multiply your sorrow and your conception; in sorrow you will bring forth children; and your desire will be to your husband, he will rule over you."

And God said to Adam, "Because you listened to the voice of your wife, and have eaten of the tree, of which I commanded you, saying, you shall not eat of it: cursed is the ground for your sake; in sorrow you will eat of it all the days of your life; Thorns and thistles will it bring forth to you; and you will eat the herb of the field; In sweat of your face you will eat bread, till you return to the ground; for out of it you were taken: for dust you are, and to dust you will return."

Imagine life without the stress of taking care of the family, with no mortgage payments or rent, no utility bills, no taxes, no grocery bills, no need for insurance, no sickness, no death... just life and living. Now the man made the choice to listen to his woman over God, but the reality is he listened to Satan over God! Because his wife was uncovered and unprotected, the man did the responsible thing. He stepped up to the plate, realizing, while he was at work, his woman was unoccupied. She was left wide open for the devil's playground. Adam proved his love for his wife Eve. He was willing to eat knowing that he would die, but he was willing to die with her than to live without her.

Imagine if the power of their unity was used for an example of relationships in life! This is the true love story of a man who did not protect his wife and tried to make it right, although he went against God. This is the account of the first man, Adam. He was tested with the WIFE! Jesus is called the second or last man, and he is tested with the Mother! You see, these two women are the most POWERFUL influences in the world! This is why she is the target of the hate and deception of the serpent! Every man is the product of a woman, but mostly one or both of these two. Every great man will acknowledge in most cases, his mother or wife and sometimes both. Sadly, though, most mother-in-laws and daughter-in-laws don't get along. Look at the potential power to have the support of the mother and the wife with no strife but unity. This equals "Power!" So we need to ask the Lord, the One who made us, to open our eyes to the truth! We have been fighting against our Help! The woman needs to understand this; we have a real enemy and a woman is not it! Your enemy hates you, and will do anything to destroy you and your future. The woman's purpose is far greater than the natural eyes can see; you must see the soul of the woman. She's gentle by nature until she's tampered with. So many women have the potential for greatness but are contaminated with pains of the past. A woman's true enemy is her spirit, sending her the worst kind of partner, one to use her and drain her of her strength to fulfill her destiny. Abused women in turn, sometimes abuse their children, not intentionally of course but when life starts dealing them a hand they didn't expect, panic and fear can take over, so they respond with anger and live their lives hurting others.

What happens when a young single mother has a baby and the baby's father doesn't love her? How about when a woman thinks having a baby will save her relationship? The baby's job is to try and keep the two of you together. How about when he loves the baby and hates the mother? This is a gateway for the evils to consume this young mother with bitterness, lack of forgiveness, and resentment. She has too much on her plate and most times shuts down because she doesn't want to be exposed or display her feelings. She already feels degraded. So she internalizes the situation. What about the women who have been abused and never ever received therapy? They go through life feeling incomplete all the time. The first person a young girl would like to confide in is her mother, but sadly, many mothers have their own deep and dark secrets! They are ashamed and don't want to disclose them to their daughters. Now the mother suspects that something is wrong with her child, because she can see the signs, but says nothing. In fact, she will make the daughter feel uncomfortable to even talk about it that she shuts down! Many times the single mother becomes a victim of many different men in and out of her life, because she's terrified of being alone or not loved. In many cases, the mother's boyfriend is the abuser, physically abusing the mother and sexually abusing the child. Because the mother is in the relationship, the child has no choice; she's in a relationship too! This spiritual enemy preys on this more than anything. He watches as the new victim handles their situation, the same as so many others have before them, so many generations.

When you don't talk about it and keep it a secret, Lucifer calls to his workers to attack your life. The truth is the light, which exposes this enemy. We are deceived to believe by keeping the secret we are not adding to the problem. A woman empowers him by being silent. Many moms don't even believe their daughters when they tell them how they have been violated and now the child really feels helpless and unprotected. Imagine the fear the child has when disclosing this information and the mother approaches the perpetrator and he, of course, denies the allegations and the mother is looking at the daughter in front of her man as if her child is lying. So now the daughter feels betrayed, abandoned, and ganged up on. Imagine what's going to happen to the child when the mother is not around. The child knows that they have lost while the perpetrator is gloating in their position of winning. Now the child has to grow up quickly. She's feeling alone and afraid. When the mother stays in the relationship, she sends a message to her child that she has chosen the boyfriend over the child. In any case, this is huge in our communities; new relationships from broken relationships become "Hurt People, Hurt People." One day this little girl will be a grown woman and who knows how she will handle life and her children? Will she be protective or give into her past and repeat this vicious cycle? The reality is that there is a greater enemy than what we can see. This problem of hate is real and needs to be dealt with. We need to deal with the root and not the fruit. Fruit is what we can see, but the root is something we can't! Fruit is produced from the root. Where is this hate coming from? Who or what is behind a grown person sexually abusing a baby or child?

What would cause a grown man to leave his woman in bed and creep in the bed with a child to sexually assault her when she's defenseless? Many women have been intimidated by these horrific circumstances. This is spiritual and I'm not saying this as a scape goat for anybody, but it's a reality! We must know it's bigger than what we see. Who would be willing to take on such a feat? Somebody has to feel the calling—someone who can relate, who knows what it's like to be abused, afraid, and helpless. When a person makes it out of such horrors, they are anointed to help someone else. They have power they may not even be aware of but they'll never know unless they try! This is the trade off and reward of perseverance. It's not for them to go on with their lovely lives as if they have not gone through anything. So many women desperately need you, more than you probably ever know. We need more women to help other women. This is affecting marriages, relationships, children, and life as a whole. If we don't fix the problem, then it will destroy the potential of happiness for lives everywhere for generations to come. We push too much under the rug. This whole deal about life on earth is just that. God has a place where we don't have an everlasting rug under which to sweep our dirt. This life is for this reason—to bear witness to the truth! All who can stand the truth will hear God's voice. People are put on this earth and given unexplainable circumstances for the purpose of exposing, helping, and rescuing innocent children.

The children are seeking answers from their parents who appear to have simply allowed these things to happen. Sometimes the mothers say they felt paralyzed with fear at the time. Some say they felt like they were stuck and had nowhere to go, and seemed to be under a spell. They cannot explain why they did not come to their child's rescue. We fight sometimes and many times out of ignorance. God gives us people that have the responsibility to bring about change. We have many examples throughout history. It may seem as though no one cares or you are carrying the weight all by yourself, but the truth is there are so many others who are just like you, and you are waiting to meet each other and will know she is your true sister by sharing the same experiences. You can find refuge in this. Trust and believe that you're not in this alone.

VIII

Chapter 8: Jezebel

Who is Jezebel?

The biblical account is her most popular and notable reference, but often misinterpreted and misunderstood. When I hear people talk about Jezebel, most of the time they identify her as a prostitute; heavy makeup, short dresses or skirts, a loose woman, a seducer of sex, and not marriage material. This is so far from the truth since she's the very opposite. While we are looking for these characteristics, the real Jezebel started out as a lovely girl born of a king and living a life of royalty in a kingdom. Her father was the king of Canaan, so she was a princess, not a gold digger. She did not have to sell her body to eat and live. She was a virgin and was saving herself for the not-yet-discovered promenade husband. She is royalty, a princess, and reared in her father's kingdom. She was being prepared for greatness! She was afforded the best education available in the world. She had access to the greatest libraries, instructors, scholars, and teachers at her disposal. She was very smart, wise, intelligent, beautiful, desirable, and respected, but soon to be feared. Her father was molding her into "a force to be reckoned with."

What's dangerous about Jezebel is she knows who she is but had no clue how she would make history. She is talked about through all generations and peoples. She is not waiting to be validated by no means outside of her world; she has made herself a Queen and god, and is worshiped as such. Her father molds and shapes her to be the most lethal of all weapons: brains and beauty. Jezebel is the desired of all men but it's understood that only a few are worthy because of her status and stature. She's admired, respected, but also feared. It's important to understand her origin; born a princess and made a Queen. This woman was so focused on fulfilling her assignment and destiny that she became one with the spirit that drove and used her. She's a woman of power and authority. She is one who has committed to a relationship with the spirit of Lucifer, long before she commits to a man. She's married to Lucifer and is in a committed relationship. Now, Lucifer is able to use her as an extension of him, simply because they are one. She is a model on how a woman should be committed to her husband and marriage. She demonstrates the benefits of agreement and how powerful it is to become one. Her commitment is to spirit, not flesh. What is modeled here, is not her commitment to the husband in the flesh but her true husband, which is spirit. Lucifer is her first husband and has been with her for a long time. He's not intimidated by her having a man in body, as long as he can benefit from the relationship. She must remain faithful to their relationship at all times and not lose focus. Many women are married to a man but in reality, the marriage is in turmoil because she will always be true to the spiritual husband first; this is where her loyalty is.

The spiritual husband is with her always while the natural husband gets lost with responsibilities and sometimes distracted with other relationships, whether business or personal. This is one of the reasons, if not the most promenade, for divorces today, because she can always get a man or men to replace a man but she will not divorce her true husband... Lucifer! He promises her that he will take care of her, that she will get a better man and have a greater life without the husband. He also tells her that marriage is holding her back from the good life and how she can do better. Why be committed to this one man when you can have your pick of the crops? If women would be honest with each other and their husbands, they will tell you how they have been bamboozled! So she listens to the spirit who is her counselor and sadly, many women will even say God told them to do it. Before any woman commits to getting married, she should be sure, that she is single! Finally, since the fall of Lucifer from his throne in heaven he's found a woman he can use fully; one who is not resistant or reluctant to him. Through Jezebel, he gets to fulfill his fantasy of being a man and a woman while at the same time having his thrill of being in control. Usually, Satan shows his face to the woman, dark and cold but Lucifer is the, "glamorous, arrogant and pompous one." By the way, Satan is Lucifer's alter-ego! They are the same, but operate from two different perspectives and understand how to submit to one another, to allow the best character to come forward for the job to be well done! Imagine how he must feel to have gone through time searching for a woman that will become one with him...

a marriage! Jezebel can hear Lucifer clearer than any other woman to date and is pleased to have such a relationship. She seeks to please her husband who is with her always. As I said before, most of the time they even think it is God, because they can feel the power of their moves! It's important to know God's character; God loves, He's peaceful, caring, sacrificial, long-suffering, giving, unselfish, compassionate, giver of life, joyful, unified, a promise-keeper, protector, and shield for his own. Lucifer needs something to work with and her desire to be loved by her father will be the gateway to the "Evil One." Willing to do anything for her father the king, she sets out to meet Ahab the king of Israel. Her father needed Israel as an ally. With this being understood, her father gives her an assignment and requests her to please the king of Israel. Her mission is to cause the king to fall madly in love with her. She's willing to do anything to please her father and to rise to power. The father knows this and takes advantage of the heart of his daughter. He justifies his actions by the mere fact that one day this kingdom will be hers. She is to win King Ahab's heart and she will inevitably get the nation of Israel. She will be rebellious to her own husband as a man but will submit to other authorities in relations to her having power over men and women, usually in the home and work place. How is the woman selected to be betrothed to a demon spirit? Who will be a candidate for such a commitment? It will definitely be someone who has been a victim of circumstances, anxious or overly ambitious; most likely molestation, sexual abuse, drug abuse, alcohol abuse, verbal abuse, domestic violence, rejection, abandonment, low self-esteem, depression—these all are gateways. While seeking to please one, they will hurt another.

After being a victim, she is now ready for her true husband who is the one we cannot see but she can hear him and he is her advisor and counselor. The reason why she obeys him is because she gets results. He gives her a way out or answer to a problem or resolve. This gives her the confidence to never be the victim ever again, so now she becomes the victor by claiming many victims. Once she tastes this power, she will never be the same again. Her past memories or lowest points were a great embarrassment to her. She uses what she has learned from her past experiences as power to thrust her into her mastery and dominating position. Jezebel, at this point, is not a woman but a spirit acting as female because it is submissive to her spiritual husband. She will tell her natural husband to be quiet and then go to herself to listen to her spiritual husband. He's with her all the time and doesn't want her to be advised by no one but himself. Many women are really the victim to this evil and don't even know it because of their position of power. If she's using her power to put people in bondage rather than setting them free, it's the enemy. If everything she achieves comes from manipulation, then it's the enemy, not God. Many pastors are operating in the spirit of Jezebel while giving God the praise from their lips, but glorifying Lucifer/Satan by their works. The spirit of Jezebel is manipulation, domination, and intimidation! Many churches today are run by this spirit. Understand that it is a spirit, so if someone is hungry and desperate for position, power, and authority, then Lucifer will use male or female, it matters not—he'll use them either way. Pimps are compelled this spirit; slavery was enforced by this spirit. The slave masters operated in the spirit of Jezebel. Her greatest achievements have been by using God's name and religion as vehicles for the movement; "Selfish Gain!" Remember, Jezebel surrounded herself with godly people, even Prophets. She hired the prophets of God and offered them a salary to prophesy for her; to prophesy lies for her wealth and prosperity. This spirit is very intelligent, highly intellectual, and virtually irresistible and intriguing! Lucifer is smart, organized, charming, good-looking, beautiful, self-centered, selfish, rich, flamboyant, charismatic, murderous, articulate, a builder of greatness, and liker of nice things as in the best money can buy. While, on the other hand, Satan is ignorant, cunning, slick, ruthless, loud, outspoken, dirty, selfish, self-centered, coldhearted, openly cruel, a killer of everything and anything, and a destroyer of anything good. Lucifer and Satan are the same being with split personalities. Jezebel works for both personalities. While Lucifer doesn't like to get his hands dirty, he will pay someone to do his dirty work for him. Satan loves dirt and that is why these two personalities get the job done; they know how to submit to one another. One is a murderer dressed with elegance and education, who kills by using a pen, and cunning by having the law on his side. The other will put on a ski mask, rob you, and simply blow your brains out. This is the same fallen angel, not two but one, working the schizophrenia. The spirit of Jezebel worships money and things bought with money; Baal. Elijah the prophet and Jezebel were arch enemies because the true prophet is not for sale and would not sell out! How many leaders do we have who started out one way and ended up another simply because of the "love of money!"

The Prophet Elijah killed 450 prophets of the Lord who

sold out to Jezebel. Elijah had trained these men for the service of God. Jezebel loved temple worship. She also loved surrounding herself with prophets and men of great influence. She would use her influence over the prophets to speak a word to the people who believed in God and His prophets. She was smart enough to submit and be obedient to the voice that guided her. It informed her of how the people would not listen to her but they would listen to their God. So she used prophets who were supposed to be men of God, who represented God. This was how she controlled the people without them feeling controlled. She is a master manipulator. They served her, believing to be doing God's service. Instead of making slaves through bloodshed and war, Jezebel with great charisma, made them slaves through religion and worship. She was very charismatic and persuasive in getting the people to give offerings to Baal. But, truthfully, everything was for the queen; she was their god but they didn't know this. They got caught up into wanting to please the queen. The people wanted to give because it pleased Jezebel to receive gifts, whether in or out of the temple. They did not want to experience her wrath! They wanted to keep her happy. The people just wanted to serve God but, deceptively, Jezebel would offer to them the God of her choice... herself! She would dress herself in such apparel that the people adored and admired her, and wanted to be like her. Women saw her beauty and strength and desired to be like her. She brought a different element to the land. Women were not accustomed to seeing this kind of power from a woman. She had King Ahab wrapped around her finger.

Now be reminded, Jezebel had no clue as to how powerful

and gifted she was. Ahab gave her the confidence because she was just trying to please her father as she attempted to please her husband. Her expressed love for her husband was not love at all, but an art as it turned into power. Once Jezebel experienced the seducing power she had over people with mind games and sex, a monster was born, and there would be no looking back for her. The once fragile, intimidated young woman afraid to leave home to go to a foreign place, was now the dominating force to be reckoned with in all the land. She used her influence to get whatever she wanted and desired. She was a different kind of queen and not just a figurehead as so many before her, but a real decision-maker behind the scenes and out front. With false humility as her covering, she was exalted to the heavens. She was now solely the initiator for wars on hand. She used her husband, the king's, signet ring to sign documents for engaging war or peace. Even King Ahab was recognizing that he was out of his league with her. He found himself in wars with his former allies because of her secret practices of unauthorized and misappropriated power. She was forging her husband's signature and using his credit to establish her own. She was taking land and properties at will and even killing all those who opposed her. She was making decisions solely on how she felt or perceived a situation. She was full of lust for stuff and could never get enough. Now the Kingdom of Israel was in her total control.

King Ahab soon became just a figurehead. He was stripped of his manhood and portrayed power only when he was away from her presence. His men knew he was weak, a poor example, but dared not say anything, for they too feared Jezebel's wrath! Jezebel's spirit was all over the land, even in households. Women were feeling somewhat inspired by this tyrant. They didn't agree with many things that Jezebel may have done but they were somewhat intrigued by her influence and power. Women were battling their prejudice of her being of another culture, race, or people versus the power they were feeling in their own households because of this foreigner. Women were not accustomed to having such power or say in the home. She was suddenly becoming every woman's dream and hero while being every man's greatest fear and nightmare. You did not want to make the terrible mistake by going against her. All who voted or supported her were rewarded and acknowledged; this was a great payoff and word spread quickly. If you did not agree keep it to yourself, there was no benefit in rebuttal. Now Jezebel was the head of the household and of Israel. What was so disturbing for Ahab was that he didn't see it coming. While Ahab was the beneficiary of seductive pleasures, his wife was taking over his kingdom. While sleeping after a mind-blowing session of wild-like passions, Ahab was getting the kingdom and his life sucked right out of him. Their marriage aside, royalty had such modest, traditional marital beginnings yet now his wife was the power that was feared and had the most influence in the land. She was now the poster for the saying, "What's Yours Is Mine and What's Mine Is Mine!" Lucifer is proud of her. She's the closest representation to date of who he is in a natural terrestrial being. This is how he wanted to operate and take over in heaven, when he said, "I will set my throne above the throne of The Most High God!"

To take over a kingdom or house you must first bind up or shut down whoever is supposed to be in charge. This is why God describes King Ahab as a disgrace, a poor example of a man and king. The fall of Lucifer was because he challenged God on how He did things. The devil did not agree with God on many subjects but God knew that Lucifer's selfish decision-making and behavior was destructive and had no longevity for life. The spirit of Lucifer in the person of Jezebel was self-centered and selfish. She cared about no one but herself. She was ruling Israel and Canaan. She was the successor of her father's kingdom and the ruler of Ahab's kingdom. The spirit of Jezebel would destroy anything that it couldn't control or subdue. Anyone who resisted would be made an example out of; do not go against Jezebel by any means or suffer the consequences. This spirit had been around for a long time. It worked through people and circumstances. It showed itself in marriages, businesses, governments, churches, and even slavery! We are often misled by titles and positions, but the wisdom of God suggests for us to be aware of the spirit that is in operation; it's when we become one with a greater power than what we see. People can be driven by this power of good or evil and know that it's something greater than themselves. How many times has a person admitted of how they were caught up or beside themselves when performing or making a speech? What about this one, "I didn't do anything; I'm innocent!" Spirits are present looking for partners to get the job done and declare who belongs to them.

It is a battle of kingdoms right here on earth. Jezebel was building up Israel for herself by importing the wealth to her god, "Baal." She was building up her god, who you can see, and tearing down Israel's God who they cannot see, because He is spirit. She feels that they are foolish to serve an unseen god because the Canaanites worship only things of "value;" tangible things, gods who are seen. So she gave them a god they could see; "Show me the money!" She taught them that if you have money you have everything and if you don't, then you are nothing. So she released a spirit in the land to do whatever you need to do to get the money. Bring her a portion of it and she will praise you before all the people as to how great you are, also it gave them hopes of being with her and being like her... treacherous. She controlled and put leaders over them with seducing spirits, making them feel good but not changing their lives for the better. Many of our leaders are anointed from the church house to the court house and government but have been rejected by God with that same anointing because they use it to do evil. Make no mistake about it, leaders are anointed whether in church or not. Lucifer was anointed long before church worship. Please understand this. Until the fall of angels and then the fall of mankind, there was no need for church or religion. It was about relationships and it still is! The purpose of any so-called religion was and is, to get back in relationship with God the father, not getting trapped in some kind of ritual cultism.

There is nothing new under the sun. Lucifer is the master over fallen angels while Satan is the master over demon spirits. Both of these spirits operate in pride, hate, and rebellion against God. Neither Lucifer nor Satan have the gift of repentance. The sign of one operating in this spirit; they are never wrong, will not apologize for anything, will not repent or turn from their evil—they lack the ability to do so. They are full of pride. On purpose, God commanded Moses to have seven days of unleavened bread after the Israelites were set free after over 400 years of bondage and slavery, so they would remember where they came from and were not slaves only because God delivered them. The enemy would have never let them go out of the kindness of their heart. He asked this as remembrance of Him and them; to show their children humility no matter how much substance they would recover or be blessed with on the 14th to the 21st day of first month of the year, each year. To eat bread with no yeast, or flat bread, to remember when they were slaves and their bread did not rise because they could not afford yeast. It was a distinction of a slave's meal. God called this His Passover and to remember the blood of the lamb that was shed for them and put over the lintel of their doorways.

Remembering the last plaque, He had smitten their enemies with killing the first born of each household. God sent a plaque in the form of the Death Angel. God made it this simple, "Where the blood is at the door don't strike but PASSOVER them." So they celebrated this ceremony from that year up to the time Jesus came and presented himself as that Passover Lamb. They saw a man; heaven saw The Lamb. When we have communion we need to reconnect to the root of why we have symbolic blood and body in the form of wine and bread.

Jezebel is in many disguises. That spirit gets over especially when you limit it to a woman. No! It is controlling, a liar, possessive, dominating, insecure, desperate for attention, and manipulative. Dressed up on the outside and messed up on the inside. If we practice serving rather than always wanting to be served, we may have hope for healing of the worst pandemic ever to hit heaven... Pride! Jezebel's most powerful companion, trust and believe it, is *pride*.

IX

Chapter 9: The Woman

When God was ready to produce life, He created His partner... the Woman!

The repairer, the fixer, the life giver, created on purpose to add and multiply until her enemy introduced her to subtraction and division.

The woman; who is she? Where did she come from? She has something to do with everything unrevealed. What a mysterious and majestic but sometimes complicated creature. She is the conduit and giver of life, partner of the producer of life.

Most of the greatest moments and memories in life are accredited to the woman. Some, if not the greatest influences and inspirations for art, music, poetry, songs, and the good things in life are to her credit. How we work, play, dress, eat, and interact is surrounded by her. The woman is the birthing place for love. The created "Producer" turned "Consumer!" How did this happen? These and other questions we will address while undertaking this journey.

She is something far above precious stones and material

things. She's not like any other creature or creation. She's more than pretty looks, a great body, a sex object or servant and definitely was not created to be enslaved by anyone or anything. She is a voice that should be heard from a different perspective and is in desperate need to be heard.

A woman is a giver of life and love; a heart fixer. Perhaps if misguided or mistreated, she become a "heartbreaker."

If trapped, she usually carries secrets throughout her life. Anything from infidelity, molestation, rape, abuse, unwanted pregnancies, abortions, carrying the secrets of how she conceived a baby out of an affair, to have a man raise a child knowing the child is not his. These are just some of the things a woman can carry sometimes all the way to her grave.

She may be a leader, adviser, friend, partner, companion, comforter, cousin, aunt, sister, girlfriend, wife or mother, good or bad. Can she be replaced? Will she be replaced? If so, who could or would try to replace her? What is this jealousy of her? Would love or life be in the world without her? How could we reproduce without her? We would be extinct. Who is like the woman in comparison?

Imagine the world without a single woman. Would a man still want to be successful or as ambitious? What about the arts? What would we write or sing about? What would be our subject matter? Would the world be as advanced? Is there anything else in existence, which is loved and hated, admired but envied at the same time?

Is there anything that can bring more pleasure or pain? Is there any other creature that could make you want to live or die for? What a creation!

Would we do the same foolish things to impress or make

the same mistakes? What would be our plot for infidelity? Would we be as competitive or motivated? Would society be satisfied having a man in her place or a for-men-only environment?

Can anyone possibly take the place of the woman? She is love and without her we would not know it or have experienced it to the fullest. Unfortunately, the flip side to all of this is the woman is the target for abuse such as rape and molestation at a very early age.

She's exposed as an innocent little girl to domestic violence. As she grows, she is exposed to alcohol, drugs, rape and physical and mental abuse. She is betrayed and sold into slavery, and trafficked as sex slaves. She deals with the epitome and personification of rejection, pain, and abandonment. She can be weak and, at the same time, the strongest at surviving and coping with unbearable circumstances. No matter her race, religion, social status, or class, she is relentless in character while still nurturing.

Why is she the target of violence, sex, and hate crimes especially if left unprotected? There is a consistent prowler on the loose and he's after all generations. There are so many victims raised in the absence and presence of a loving father. Do you know the devil got Eve while Adam was at work? What is the driving force behind this abhorrence? To find the answer, let's take a journey back to the beginning before the woman existed. What is the reason for her creation, her purpose? Why the hate for her? Who would hate such a lovely creation that can make life so good? Why turn her evil? Why use her for evil? Why manipulate her? If she is evil, what happened? Was she always this way or did a series of events shape her into this thing? Why do we so lustfully look at her physical shape and outer appearance? She has so much more that most never get to see. This is her God part. It's on the inside... her mind. This is not the original creation.

The greatest contributors and influences in this world are women. But the mother and the wife need to recognize their greatness. If they love you and are for you, they can be the greatest things to ever happen to you, but on the other hand, if they are against you, nothing and no one but God can help you.

Why is it that for the most part, the mother-in-law and daughter-in-law don't get along? Why are they mostly at odds? The reason is that the seed (son) is the center of the woman's divine calling. The battle began with prophecy regarding the seed.

For the mother, he is the hope of her future, to deliver her. She hopes he will remember how she protected and nurtured him when he was unable to take care of himself. To the wife, he is her man, her lover, provider, protector and potential father of her children. He is her everything! A man; not somebody's boy.

These two women are battling over the love of one man. It's important for these two powerful women to know and understand that they need each other in ways not imaginable. If they come together in agreement, there are no limits.

One sees him as her child, while the other sees him as her man. They both stake the claim of knowing him and of course the mother feels she knows him the best. The mother, who raised and nurtured him feels justified at best. But the wife is feeling something totally opposite. To her, he is not a child.

Well maybe sometimes a bit childish, but at any rate a man... her man!

These two power sources are greater than they know sometimes. The mother should understand the wife's feelings and the wife should try to understand the mother's feelings.

Why? Because the mother with the son, more than likely at one time or another, was under pressure of being accepted.

Many women get caught up in relationships that are going nowhere. The misunderstanding is this; just because you meet on the same road, doesn't mean you are going in the same direction or headed to the same destination in life. It used to be the woman was being in it for the long haul; she's on the interstate, while a guy may be on the road until he comes to the next exit or two. When she looks around, he is gone and she then picks up the next one on the road. She's just a little farther along on her journey and a little scornful each time she picks up another traveler.

This is a great misunderstanding. These should not fight at all, but humble themselves to and for a greater calling; to help to encourage, fortify and help to shape this man for greatness. Helping according to the will of God and to the fulfillment of divine purpose and destiny. Most of us live for our time on earth without the understanding of the bigger picture, which is eternal life.

We are sowing seeds here for a greater harvest there. The love of a mother and wife are two most distinctive loves; one totally different from the other. The love was customized for the two, and never meant to be the same love. Love is never meant to be compromised, but given to the maximum, because they are two completely different kinds of love but uniquely shared.

Just think about it for a minute. From the beginnings of Adam and Eve, when they were in the Garden of Eden, to the humble beginnings of a child being born in a little town of Bethlehem. This virgin birth changed life as we know it forever and started time over from B.C. to A.D. to present since his days on earth. What year is this, or what do we call it? Actually giving birth to greatness is a common part of her very existence. Think of every great leader and life changer, whether good or evil, small or great; they came through a woman!

How about the woman who has given up on love because of her past hurts and disappointments? She is an easy target for pimps, scammers, and hustlers. It's easy to use her, manipulate and control her. Usually the perpetrator looks for this kind of woman. He is skilled and trained to cater to her insecurities without seeming to even notice she's insecure.

He's often persistent and appears kind and overly understanding. This will cause an inexperienced woman to let her guard down and allow him into her life. He will give her things in the beginning as bait to win her over. Most times, what he has was acquired from other women. Some women may be the same, but if so, it's because of the past hurts caused by a man.

Every human being is here because a woman somewhere gave her life to give life! Man has the seed and it needs to be planted to bring forth life, for life depends on the woman and where that seed is planted then produces life.

Who else shapes and molds the course of history and its

greatness? Be it in the confines of a small house cooking dinner or bathing her children while getting them ready for bed
or the world stage. Maybe even sending the children off to
school, helping them with their homework, while working
two or three jobs to make ends meet. These are the many natural facets of the woman. From work to play, she is a force to
be reckoned with.

She is challenged in many ways, sometimes, unimaginable
ways, from the beginning of her life. She holds so many secrets that she dares not think to share. As much as she gives,
she holds back so much for fear of being judged or frowned
upon. Some of her experiences have been so shameful that she
would never tell a soul. No matter how close you may think
you are to her and no matter how much you may think you
know about her, she still holds things in her mind and heart
as a safe place.

She gives so much of herself, and by doing so she holds
potential or greatness in her arms. It doesn't matter if she is
feeding with milk from her own breasts, giving herself away
for the sake of so many others. She represents the nature of
God in many ways. She is nurturing by nature, whether it is
the next president or mass murderer, her love, for the most
part is unconditional.

Look at successful men over the years and when it's time
to give thanks, recognition or honor the first thing no matter
how old the male is, you will hear, "Hey Mom or thanks Mom,
I love you Mom." No matter how much the father has con-
tributed and provided for, it doesn't matter. His very nature
and or spirit is reaching out to the mother from within.

That's why most men who have not had a relationship or

had a bad relationship with their mother are underachievers! The woman is the most powerful creature to date in this present world.

But now, she must be heard loud and clear through her own voice. She has to be brought to the light to help fix this problem the world is having. It's going to take all the women of the world to fix the problems we've got. It needs to be a global effort! The serpent targeted the woman from the beginning and she will be heard in the end! If those who oppose evil will not give her a platform to be heard, the serpent surely will. When the church told her to be quiet, the world gave her a horn! Should we, who say we are the leaders of God, give her the right to be heard, since in the scriptures, we see how the enemy hates her? We are to teach and protect her. We are not controlling her, but assisting her as guiding lights in this dark world. Again, I'm not empowering the serpent in the woman, but the God in her; there is a difference. When a woman is faithfully working to bring good to any situation, she should be heard, supported, and confident. Are we hypocrites, afraid of change? We will use her for evil but we need her input for good, we need her for change. The earth will listen to her; the Word of God says so. "And the earth helped the woman and swallowed up the flood, that the serpent sent, to carry the woman away." All creations are in pain, waiting for the woman to be revealed. Women are working overtime on their outer appearance, and not investing much into the heart. She can't fulfill her purpose carrying all of that hurt and pain! We are encouraging her to be vain; "eye candy!" But she's more than that! Maybe we are partially responsible by denying her as a voice. She has to be heard one way or another. This is who she is, and we need to take more time to know her. Out of hurt and pain, many turn to the extreme, where they can express themselves; the strip club! Now here's a place where she can be heard. She controls this house and is worshipped. She dresses and then undresses, and money is thrown on the stage while she's dancing. The more she takes off, the more money is laid at her feet. This is one of her voices. Many of these women are victims of sexual abuse. Many have been molested or raped. Who can she go to and tell her true story? Some will take back the power of those who took her voice (body). Since you won't hear what I have to say, then see how I can get my prey! She knows how to get her prey! So many are bitter and angry. Many come from church and other places where they weren't heard. I'm not saying all, but many are what they call "backsliders." I've met quite a few in my day. Many have said they don't see much difference in how they get their money versus a misguided preacher getting his or hers. It is a seducing spirit. We do need to recognize this spirit. If a preacher is getting money the way a stripper does, then it is a seducing spirit. Both of them are selling something they know they can't deliver. Legally, an "exotic dancer" must obtain a license for dancing. She understands that she is not licensed to sell sex. Exotic dancers are selling fantasies and are paid well for it. The better they paint the picture, the more they get paid. The money starts to pile up if she's a good storyteller with her body.

The devil puts so much attention on her body that the majority misses out on her mind. An educated woman who is also a woman of God meaning she will not be used for wickedness and evil. Many women have walked away or lost jobs because they would not bow to the world and the church. I'm definitely not talking about rebellion. "Rebellion is as witchcraft."

We will see in the end that the woman will be restored to her rightful place of royalty and righteousness. The world will not recover until she repents and turns back to her God who loves her and created her from that love. Love is her power and majesty, not hate or lust.

Look at how far the woman has come up in every genre and industry in just one hour (from 1960 to 2020; 60 years). God calls 60 years one hour in the book of Revelation. She has made more progress and accomplished more than the beginning of time. No matter how hard she is oppressed. This is her season and time to be vindicated. The heavens are echoing her victories. Be sure to be Mary having lambs and Jezebel birthing goats. Sheep follow and goats rebel. God will be with you for the good. Making this world a better place, allow God to use you. After all, He is the one who created you. Satan wants to use you up and make a mockery of you as well as your seed. If you remain partners with God not only will you be anointed but the world will see God's glory on your life to be the problem solver rather than the problem.

Like it or not... the world is changing and has changed! God is calling the woman not to be bossy but to be a boss. This is your time to show the universe that you remember who you are and that you are the chosen replacement. It was so necessary then and now for your unveiling. By all means do not be partners with your enemy but your God who created you.

God bless the Woman!

X

Chapter 10: Who Am I?

"These things must come to past but pray for your journey."

What does this question mean? It simply means in heaven and eternity certain things had taken place or was concealed in a heart and must be exposed in a realm where it could be annihilated. A thought is a thought but when meditated upon, it is transferred to the heart. Iniquity was found in the heart of Lucifer; evil and good will have to be exposed. It's like surgery; it may hurt for a while, but the ultimate goal is to save your life, so we cut to save, not destroy. God is saying, "I know it will hurt but we have to get to the bottom of this." There was a lot of scheming and plotting going on in heaven behind God's back—*hypocrites.* Pretending to love God when, in reality, they loved all of the gifts and things more than God. They were willing to do whatever it took to have power, glory, and control even if it meant killing God! There were so many plans that were interrupted, it's unbelievable!

Who can know the heart but God? Similar to the movie

The Matrix, if someone dies they would be dead for real. If Lucifer would have killed God in eternity, then God would have been dead for real—forever! Now imagine Lucifer as the God of all gods. This evil in the world was really Lucifer's plan outside of God's plan. He really believed to have had a better system and way of life than God but lacked the insight, vision, education, and experience to think it through above his level. Now, he's smart and is no dummy, but creation and organizing the universe is definitely out of his league. Truthfully even Lucifer didn't know it would have turned out this bad. All the evil, wars, death, and misery are a result of a selfish plan by the devil without thinking or seeing it through responsibly or intelligently. This is an eternal lesson we are still learning in time; listen to someone who has the experience and has been where you are trying to go. But since it was in Lucifer's heart, God cannot ignore what He sees. He is now responsible for its release, and to get rid of it, like a bomb squad. God put him out of heaven to allow the explosion and exposure of his plan. God would not judge him on foreknowledge; this would not be fair. But for the safety of all life, it must run its course. Lucifer's argument could have been, "Yes I've thought about it, but I would never actually do it!" God knew he would and it was only a matter of time. So, in God's infinite wisdom, He creates a module of time and casts the terrorists in it. Satan is our first terrorist! Satan again is Lucifer's "ultra-ego." Lucifer is the politically correct one while Satan is the wild, ruthless, openly cold, blunt, dark, and wicked one. Satan is the hood-rat, the gangster, the street thug, the rapist, and the dark cold killer. Lucifer is cool, classy, sophisticated, charismatic, charming, educated, patient, calm, and seductive. He looks good and is easy on the eyes, but is more lethal than his ultra-ego. He kills by the masses with deception of charm and seduction. Unfortunately, there are some innocent people who have nothing to do with this, but have been infected by Lucifer's deception. God has to have a plan for those who are innocent and declares the difference between all of those who are weak or wicked—sheep or goats. The weak can be made strong and belong to God while on the other hand, no matter what, the wicked will never turn from their evil ways; they belong to Satan. The strong, in destroying hope and life, are Satan's property. The sheep belong to Christ and the goats belong to Lucifer. These have two very distinct natures and characteristics. Lucifer uses the woman because he knows that she is God's most prized possession and greatest agent. Remember, he saw her as his replacement while he was falling. The woman is no joke, but the problem is she doesn't know her value. She was created as royalty, ruler of the gold; she didn't have to dig for it. The wealth that Lucifer had in heaven came from her kingdom of God. Lucifer is beneath her, but she doesn't know her worth. Satan pimps her, sometimes as a whore walking the streets or through Lucifer in the corporate world. How about the government? Nonetheless, this is done without her knowing who she is and whose she is; she will get burned. Lucifer/Satan cannot get the job done of destroying the world without the woman. Women, ask yourselves these questions, "Who am I and what is my worth?"

What are my roles in movies or in music? What about your role in music videos, or the subject in a song, or the role in education? Am I a voice to be heard or taken seriously in the household? What about marriage? How about divorce?

What role do you hold in all of this? How many strip clubs are you in? What is your role? How many do you own? How many women sell their bodies and reap the harvest? Why do women cheat with married men and then when they get married hope to have a faithful husband? Why do single and married women sleep with married men? Why do women spend their money and support the music industry that degrades them and calls them out of their names? Isn't this sick? Think about it! Would music even sell if all the women around the world demanded respect and a change? I can tell you this, a man is not and will not listen to a song with a bunch of men talking about their cars, houses, ice, clothes, and drinks without *women*; this is for sure. Wake up, ladies, wake up! God created you for His glory and not Satan's foolishness. He created you to destroy Satan's works, not build them up. Satan is your enemy and he is using you to build his kingdom and having you fight each other and compete with one another. You are the greatest and you need to know it; be confident not arrogant, always use yourself to God's plan and glory and be at peace with it. Come out of depression over someone not knowing your value; know your own value.

Have you ever had a good man who gave you everything when you knew you didn't deserve it, and one day he revealed to you of your infidelities, put you out, and replaced you? Well, this is the pain Lucifer just can't get over. Girlfriend, he hates you. He became jealous of the woman and was replaced by her. This birthed a new characteristic that came out of him. He had a secret and it was exposed. He thought he was irreplaceable and found out that it was a lie. He wished he could look like her and work it like her; he wished he were her. He fell from a god to a dog, God backwards! If you listen when someone is saying it, you will hear its origin, "Lucifer the Fallen!" He envied her everything from the moment he saw her. So let me challenge you with this question, who is calling you a dog? Answer; Lucifer, Satan, and the Devil! Women don't let the "B's" confuse you. Lucifer was a god in heaven, who became the "b***h" that was cast down to the earth, who became the "burden," who used to be "blessed." So don't accept anyone calling you a "B" unless they mean blessed! The Angel said to Mary, "All the nations of the world will call you blessed!" Women, it's time to know who you are! He is using any vessel and person that he can use, anyone they can speak through, anything they can express themselves through, such as a man, a woman, a friend, a foe, a girlfriend, a boyfriend, a husband, a wife, a father, a mother, a brother, a sister, a cousin, an uncle, an aunt, boss, co-worker, classmate, schoolmate, roommate, an ex-mate, an inmate, radio, TV, music, and digital and social media—get the picture, anything and anyone who they can use to get the point across! Don't support them and God knows you should not agree with them!

This is their deception and sometimes it's so subtle. Remember this word, subtle. When the serpent was with Eve in the Garden of Eden, he was *subtle*. He was "delicately complexed, especially of a change or distinction, so delicate or precise as to be difficult to analyze or describe." Your enemy is good at this! When the serpent talked to Eve, he made her feel and think that she was missing something or in need of something. He proposed to her that if she ate of this tree, she would be like God. She was already like God but did not know who she was. The woman created by The Most High

God as a Queen and she needs to know this; "You are nobody's dog!" Most people used by the Devil will ease the word in, especially if not challenged. This suggests that it's okay and they will continue to use it on a consistent basis. This devil is so bold because of the women's support (when you say nothing or do nothing, then you are supporting). He degrades her openly and publicly, even in the music lyrics and you are his greatest sales. Why would a woman, any woman, listen to a song that is calling her out of her name and putting her down? Get this, she is in the video beside the vessel that the Devil is speaking through, sending his message to the world with her assistance as a visual display of agreement and she is under his spell helping him to build his kingdom, destroying the lives of young girls, who will one day be *women*. Damaged goods because of you! *Wake up*! How do you think God feels (yes, God has feelings) about His daughter, the queen, princess, being called a *dog*? This is total disrespect and those who are doing it without repentance will answer one day to the King! One might ask, who would treat the woman like this; who's a potential mother, wife, daughter, sister, aunt, cousin, and friend? Your enemy! Do you know why? Because he hates you! He will use anyone, anybody, and anything to get that point across to you and the entire world! Some will of course use it with anger and force! The Devil is saying, "I will keep calling you a dog until you believe it; I will keep calling you a dog until you agree with me. I'll even make you think that it's *cute* to accept it!" It's cool... it's hip-hop slang!

When God created you, He made you a "god" and the serpent flipped that thing around in the garden and made you a "dog." Satan got the world going backwards and has the woman thinking it's the good thing to be. You must know that it's not God calling you dog after the availability of salvation! We may have been a dog after the fall of man, but after the work of Calvary, the reconciliation and restoration of mankind, we don't have to be anybody's dog anymore. Lucifer's spin on this is, "You don't know who you are and I hate you, simply because God loves you! Every woman is on my hit list!" God has given you the *power* and the *glory* to run this world. He also blessed you to build up His kingdom. Women, you must work together and not against each other. "I'll never allow you to work together," your enemy is talking to you. The angels in heaven worked in "Legions" meaning; many working together as one, usually about 6,000 angels!

Legion is not a bad name or even a demonic name, but a kingdom method of dispatching a unit to get the job done, having no division; the state of being single-minded. There were legions of angels who were single-minded with God and there were also angels who were single-minded with Lucifer. So there were countless of angels cast down into the earth and decided to work together as legions. Lucifer was wise enough not to abandon this method and system of work since it has proven itself as being the most effective in getting the job done. Even if it is evil, the principle for achieving successful results remain the same. Working in agreement is a godly principle. A legion is working together in agreement at all times to complete an assignment. This was their training and skills as angels. They know the power of agreement! We as married couples, family, church, community, government, and a nation could really learn from *legion*. That's why the Devil gets so much more done than the church and religion; because we are distracted and divided over the simplest things. Religious beliefs, religions, traditions, even denominations, are just foolishness and Satan is cracking up and does not care about our gathering together just as long as we do not agree.

"*Stay in those walls while I have the streets, industry, entertainment, corporations, businesses, your families and all that you love and desire. When I know who I am as a woman then and only then no one can disrespect me or keep me from reigning.*" You've been lied to for too long. In the end who do you think God will use to heal the world? "*It started with me and I will restore what was broken after healing my brokenness by not tearing my sisters down. Now, I can see me and know who I am.*"

XI

Chapter 11: Damaged Goods

Why is the woman hated so much? Where is the hate coming from? A young, beautiful woman is single and lives with her mom who is also single. It's a nice sunny afternoon and she's outside for some fresh air. She's young and has just finished high school. She's got her whole life ahead of her whatever that may entail. She sees a man, very handsome and a little older than her, but she's curious and intrigued. He's got a car, a very nice car. This is definitely a good catch, she's thinking. She makes herself noticeable. He notices her and begins to talk. "Would you like a ride?" She's excited, but plays it cool, because she doesn't want him to think she's desperate. They have some conversation and get something to eat; they are having a good time. She's excited about her time with this man. He's making her feel like a woman. He comes around again and she's really excited to see him; no faking this time. When they go out this time, she feels it's time; a woman knows, it can't be explained. The guy is ready and gets this "pretty young thing" but he left out one small detail. Now he's fulfilling lust and she's giving love, at least that's what she thinks. She is too young to know what love is, how could she know? She was not raised by her father. These two different dynamics are where the potential of hurt and destruction lie. They continue to see each other without knowing it's from two different perspectives. But at this point, who cares? It's about to go down; one is very experienced and the other is coming into herself and nervous. She just wants to please him more than being pleased, but she can't help but wonder, "Will he like it? Am I good enough?" Soon enough she will become a much excepted statistic in her community. Shortly after, she discovers that she is pregnant and she's only eighteen years of age. Now she has to break this news to the guy first and then her mother. She breaks the news and he tells her that he is married and already has a child; he cannot be with her like that. She gets a broken heart along with broken dreams. She's thinking, how could something that felt so good, turn so quickly and hurt so bad? Now another young woman has to carry the weight of being a mother before she can even put her own life in motion and on course. Now the same man that brought her joy and excitement is now her greatest distress; the dream is turning into a nightmare. The nightmare is a familiar one, but it's new to her. The story is an old one but played to a new audience. History repeats itself but we have been taught to hide our flaws and falls because we see it as shame. Therefore, we don't share our experiences because we simply want to be accepted, loved, and respected. So fear is used to navigate us into silence; to hide the dark secrets of our past. Seriously, who wants their past coming up in their future after growing up, trying to find your way through life, especially now, if you have a spouse and family? "Just go away," we are saying to our past because it doesn't make us look good. What if our children knew how weak or stupid we've been in our past, would they respect us then? These thoughts had created prisons of the mind for a lot of people, especially women; a living hell, almost on a daily basis. Some move on with the opposite of their experiences; some become overly protective and the children don't know why. Some live with phobias and anger, developing trust issues. Then the children, out of desperation, will often use comparisons of a friend or someone else's mother and seeing the freedom that child is living. Funny we are all different but the same in some way because of our life experiences. This is spiritual and has no limits or boundaries. Most of the time, without knowledge, we leave the next victim wide open for foul play. Not seeking to cause problems in this guy's life, she attempts to move on with the help of her mom. Now the big question, how do we handle this problem? Should the pregnancy be terminated? Of course it is a considered option; why, the man doesn't want the baby! After much pain, hurt, and consideration, another young and single woman makes the unselfish decision of compassion for a helpless unborn life; to keep the baby. This decision will follow her for the rest of her life. Now she must become a woman, ultimately, a mother! She must find work to support her child; a baby girl. Working now as a single mom, she is faced with challenges of not being able to make the necessary money with a high school diploma. She's naive and has no clue that this is an old problem happening to a new victim. The young, new mom has to let go of her dreams of going to college, at least for now, but who knows? The baby's father definitely cannot afford to deal with her because he's trying to keep his marriage. Working to provide, the young mom is challenged with making a life for her and her baby. Later, she meets a guy who appears to be a good prospect for the future for her and her child. She eventually marries and seems to be able to give her child a fair chance at having a pretty normal life. Maybe she can put an end to this vicious cycle of single moms with fatherless children; she is giving her child a chance. Like any marriage, some challenges begin to develop. The woman, who has become the mother and wife, is challenged with working long hours till the night. The husband has an appetite for TV, alcohol, a little weed, and something else, but his wife is not home. He decides to touch her baby in an inappropriate way. The thought of someone whom you trust violating your baby is appalling. It's hard enough trying to make ends meet and making countless sacrifices.

To top it off, many times the mother does not find out for years; sometimes never! Violating this poor baby will become a new formed habit. It will go on for years and the child is growing up confused and dysfunctional but thinks this is normal; everyone has problems, right? From the perspective of the child, even if they suspect some wrongdoing, they can't quite put their finger on it. From the time the child has memory to the present school age years, this has been her life. As she grows older, it becomes more difficult to live with, but who does she tell and is it her fault?

So the saga continues; the mother is working so hard that

all she wants is to take care of her family, survive, have some peace and get some rest. In the meantime, the husband is not even trying to contribute to the household but is at home drinking and watching television as a daily routine. When the daughter comes home from school, she needs to find a way to spend less and less time in the house around her stepdad. Maybe out of sight and out of mind, but little does she know, this thing is way bigger than him wanting her or having a fetish.

What's driving him or what is his goal here? Because surely, he can't see her as his woman, or can he? Now he's showing signs of obsession and even jealousy. She's a child, isn't she? This is too much for her at her age. She can't even be with her friends without him calling her into the house or finding reasons to get her away from them. He wants her all to himself, especially while her mom is away at work; any opportunity he can find. She's afraid to bathe or use the bathroom, because of the fear that he might be peeping on her. She can't help but wonder, would this be happening to her if she was his biological daughter? She's become more mature or grown than the average person, even though she does have issues. She's resentful, angry, and filled with mixed emotions. She just wants to have a normal life. She doesn't know if that's even possible. She's surrounded by chaos, and physical and verbal abuse; it's her normal. Will she ever have peace?

She's dealing with a new fear now; she has her period. She's entering womanhood now and this monster is still in her life. At this point, conflicts begin to occur because she doesn't want to be in the house without her mother being there. She feels as though she is the problem because he's describing her as being disrespectful. To her mom it appeared this way as well; that she is the problem. She stands her ground but doesn't know the outcome. All she knows is she doesn't want the baby. She's too young for all of this! What else could she do? Maybe if she got a boyfriend? She's really confused!

As she grows older, she's has confused thoughts and unanswered questions in her mind. When did all of this start and how did she get trapped in this mess? Why does she feel like she's done something wrong? This situation she's in has caused her to grow up too fast; she had to survive. She's twelve and she's never had a good night's sleep.

He deals with her as if he is her man instead of her father. She feels manipulated and controlled and she won't have it. My mom and I are going through, because I don't want to do this anymore, but how can I put it to an end? At the age of twelve I have to try to put this in perspective of how I played a part in this, am I at fault here... it's just not right? How could a man do this to an innocent child? All the child wanted was to be loved the right way. What's sad is, how can this damaged soul know what love is now? Will she recognize it when it comes? What does love look like anyway? Maybe it will never come? The hate that the enemy has for the woman is real, its spiritual and will continue to manifest in and through something as long as the earth and life remains until the day of Judgment. From the beginning, this war was initiated by the one who she replaced. She did not know anything of the previous arrangements of position she was called to fill. She just opened her eyes one day and their she was, enjoying life and suddenly interrupted with hate and war. We have no control over what race or country we are born in;

we are what God envisioned us to be. We are born with a calling no matter what the race, nationality, economic status or religion. We all are contributors to this life, whether good or evil. All women are a target for hate and hate crimes. All your enemy can see when he looks at you is, you are the one who took his place and you are the reason why he cannot be the favorite in God's life. Trust this, he's learning from you all the time hating you. The woman is crowned with the glory of God. If she will dare to submit to the One who created her for His purpose, rather than listening to the lies and deceptions of her enemy, then she will be the victor and not the victim. She can do all things and all things are possible, if she only believes. On purpose, women are born into diverse situations with dynamics of life and experiences. Each woman is equipped with something that another woman needs.

God is just, even when things may not seem fair. Since God's most prized possession became a target of hate, in turn she will be given her day of vengeance. One day the woman will be able to literally see every plot and scheme, even the people who were used by Satan working against her in her mortal life on earth. She will see how sometimes, he used family members and relationships to try and destroy her destiny and purpose. He uses a face or person you trust, only to find out, they were double agents, working against you for the devil. Just because we share the same womb, doesn't necessarily mean we are family. Sometimes we will be born with our adversaries, but our job is to love them anyway. There will be times you might have to run for your life not to violate anything with God. When you discover they are working against you and your God-given purpose then leave. It doesn't matter who they are. If they are the enemy of what God has called you to, then they are working for Satan! So many women have been damaged but are still good.

Cece Winans, one of the most loving, anointed and sincere vessels of the millennium, lends her everything to "Alabaster Box." Written by Janice Sjostan, it is definitely divinely inspired. Heaven came down to share this story in modern times through lyrics and music. This has to be one the greatest depictions of a woman who was seen by most to be the worst kind of sinner (if there is such a thing), lost having no hope, rejected, and despised. However, she pressed her way through the worst kind of hate to the greatest demonstration of forgiveness, healing, restoration, and love through Jesus **(Luke 7-37-50)**.

XII

Chapter 12: 80/20

I am called, "20."

I was supposed to be with the 80, but truthfully I was never a part of the 100 percent club. Where did I come from and where do I belong? I was conceived out of lust; my parents came together by default. They both were searching for something to fill a void. They were cheaters—the unfaithful! They couldn't be trusted; something was missing. I wasn't supposed to be here, but somehow, I'm in the middle of this mess; and while on the prowl, they selfishly made me and they don't even love me because they lusted after each other! My father was married and in love, of course this was before I was born. He was looking for a 20, because his wife was distracted by someone or something and stopped being 100 percent to him. I'm the 20 percent he found while trying to fill that void, that missing (thing) percentage. I'm hated and I didn't do anything to anybody but showed up! She was not taking care of him like she used to when they first starting dating. She changed... so this is what he says. I was conceived out of an affair... he cheated; wait, or was it my mother who cheated? I'm confused!

This I do know; I'm a "bastard." No one really loves me and I can't go home to be celebrated because I must be kept a secret. They didn't make love when they made me, but they had wild, on the fly, irresponsible, non-committed, unplanned and unprotected sex! I'm not loved. I'm telling you the truth. I'm tolerated and I'm really mad about that! They think I don't know how I got here, but I do. I don't quite understand, but when I get old enough, I will be on the prowl too... maybe when I'm a mature 20, I'll find my 80? Then maybe I can be in the 100 percent club. We'll see. Maybe I can have and be a part of a real family someday... maybe one of my own? Yes... I'll do better than they did! When two people are interested in each other, they are willing to do things on purpose to gain the attention of their partner and satisfy them. This is the hunt and the chase! They have a desire to please one another, and a willingness to spend time to evaluate each other. Depending on the discovery, this will determine if in fact this is someone you could spend some serious time with. The more interested you are, the more time you are willing to invest in the potential relationship. Somewhere along the line, someone determines the next step. If the next step is successful, it starts to progress. During this time, you find out things about each other; strengths and weaknesses. Usually during this time, everyone is putting their best foot forward and giving their best game. This is the determining factor, whether or not, if this person is "The One" or one of the ones, until you find "That One!" In many cases, honesty is determined based upon how desperate the potential date is.

Motives are very important here; this is the hardest part of the whole process. Question; are we on the same page here? There's no way to determine this without honesty and transparency. Some women will tolerate a man or partner while hoping for their true love (knight in shining armor) to come along and sometimes get caught up. The poor man doesn't have a clue; he originally was tolerated and not loved! She had zero plans of keeping him. Some say, "He grew on me. I learned to love him over time." Many times they don't even know what that is; it's an imaginative person with no flaws or issues. It can be an image of good things, times, and persons created in the imagination of a childlike mind while growing up or watching TV. Sometimes it seems as though you've somehow stumbled onto the most perfect person. The longer you are together and the more time invested, things will come out on both sides to make this journey questionable to say the least. If we are experienced, we will by nature, start comparing previous relationships or someone who we know or have come into contact with; maybe someone we admire from afar? Many times we want what we see someone else with. The problem with this is we are only seeing the part we're allowed to see. Too many times, people choose someone who is taken or spoken for, because they like what they see. Besides, someone else did all the work, they're just seeking benefits! This may not be a conscious act, but just the same; why would you deal with a man who's married? This is a hate crime... woman against woman! When you start comparing, it's not a true analysis, because it's an illusion, not reality.

What is making reality shows so popular is people's interest in something real. So when they look at a reality show, it makes them feel a part of what's going on, because they feel as though they can relate or they're seeing something they wish they could have. Even if the reality show is staged, just the thought of being allowed to follow someone's life makes you feel a part of what's going on. In other words, we are invited front and center into someone's private life and business, seeing flaws in stars! Maybe it creates the feeling that, "Well, I'm not the only one going through things, but they're supposed to be stars and look at what they are going through!" What is this feeling of getting to see behind the scenes, the life of prominent people who have been thought of as super human? We all want to relate to something real! When we finally believe that we have found that special someone, we are willing to make sacrifices to be available for him or her. Only the person can define what "special" is; beauty is in the eyes of the beholder. When they fall in love, they will do anything for their partner, if they're feeling them. Here's something every woman needs to understand, and that is, "the needs of a man." The old adage, "the way to a man's heart is his stomach," doesn't hold true! Ask any man if that's true, and if he's honest, he will tell you, that it is so far from the truth. That may have been true in the days when there was a shortage or lack of food; it seems the only plausibility. It will take a whole lot more than food to get a man's heart, and that is for sure! Now we can eat at any restaurant of his choice or from a friend and they will not have his heart, just his stomach!

Unless that man is from a faraway desert and is homeless, he can find food anywhere. But finding the love of his life and his other half is priceless and his greatest quest. When a woman has a man's heart, he will tolerate many non-pleasurable things that may come with the relationship. We are all grown here, so come on, you did not get that man with all of that drama; you strategically hid those things from him in the beginning. You were sure to schedule and manage your time around his desire to be with you. This is the stage of the hunt; chase and capture. Everyone you meet may not spark your interest, but when you find the one that does, you will and are willing to go all out for him. You will deliberately make him feel so special and important to you, that he's willing to change everything in his life for you. This is how you evaluate where the relationship is, and how far it has the potential to go. If you are feeling him and this is something you really want, you do know how to turn up the heat. Women are naturally equipped with this "skill." Your skill is what is capturing his attention and he's starting to gravitate to you even more. It cannot be explained, but somehow there's an exchange for the attention you are giving him right now. No matter how tough a man pretends to be, his greatest desire, besides hustling to make money for the lifestyle he may want to give to you, is your attention and love. Yes, this is the truth and this will work overtime, if he has potential feelings for that woman. If this is the man she wants and is feeling him in the right way as a potential partner, she is willing to do whatever it takes to gain that man. Don't be fooled by the false reports of friends saying, if that was them, they would not tolerate or put up with certain things.

Behind closed doors, everybody puts up with a portion of crap that life brings, but it's about how we handle those things. Life is about handling "crap" in some way or form. She makes him feel like a king and the most important man in the world to her. She has this kind of influence and power. If the man is really feeling her and is playing no games and is equipped, then he will reciprocate. No matter how much the woman has going on in her life, she will jungle them to meet the expectations of the new man in her life. She is a saleswoman at this time and she's selling that thing! At this point, there's nothing she will not do for him and he is leaving everything behind to be with her. He is not playing and may be getting a little too dependent and possessive over her. She has somehow become the most important thing in his life. She becomes the center of his life, and most, if not all, of his decisions are based around her. During this period, she gives him sex and love on a consistent basis; she does not miss a beat. We live in a very diverse and perplexed society. Nothing is what it used to be. If she becomes pregnant, this will change everything and most couples don't even talk about it in the beginning, especially if it was not planned. Now her body is going through all sorts of changes and emotions as well. During this period, she's learning her body as the child is developing. During this process, she's challenged to give her man the attention and time as she did before, because she has a lot going on.

This stage is very crucial and it needs to be addressed. Most times it is too sensitive to touch; many leave it alone in hopes it will fix itself. Everything today is so fast-paced and readily available. Once the man starts to feel neglected, he begins to stray and this is dangerous. Without the attention of his woman, he becomes vulnerable and an easy target for "infidelity." If this relationship is not guarded by real love, and a God conscience, cheating is almost inevitable. Again I speak from experience and not for all, but relatable cases. While pregnant the woman is going through all kinds of changes that she doesn't understand. Her appetite is changing and is having less desire for sex, at least for some women. In reality, what is your man doing during this period; because that is just what it is, a period... everything has stopped in the love and affection department. We need to be real to have a resolution. He is going crazy, trying to accommodate her and is failing miserably. Now he has needs and they are not being met. This is where hypocrisy comes into play, because usually the woman doesn't want to talk about it or isn't willing to do anything. She's going through changes and rightfully so. The man is about to make a bad move, if he hasn't already. His woman, who was his "100" is now an "80." He's so desperate and deprived, that any woman who's willing to give him some attention or what he's been missing will get this man, even if for one night. The reality is, he's missing the 20 percent that he's accustomed to getting from his own woman.

He may be thinking, "I was just horny and I had to get some," but if it was better than expected, he will return for more. This can be lethal because of the betrayal. He may not intend for it to go that way, but anything can happen when that door of unfaithfulness and betrayal is open. Now the "side piece" becomes closer than planned. This is a problem, because his woman is still in love and is carrying his baby. She is not drifting, but feeling joy awaiting the arrival of their new addition to the family. The woman's enemy is all in the mix of things. Her enemy (serpent) is talking to her man every chance he can get. It is putting things in his ear on a consistent basis. Communication is vitally important but who has the wisdom to know this? While somebody in the relationship is chasing the 20 or the missing part in his life, the enemy has a plan greater than what appears to be missing. It's about the destruction of the family and having total access to the unborn baby (seed). While all of these elements are appearing to have validity, something has a bigger plan and it's about destroying life and happiness, though it started out just seeking a good time... the "20." Once trust is broken, evil can take hold, because it has been given rights to the lives on all parties—including the unborn baby. The sad thing is; this family had so much potential, but by not watching and covering each other, the enemy came in like a flood. With so many problems and distractions, it's almost impossible to fix them. Some have made babies out of this confusion during the affair. Look at how this affects the life of unborn children.

In most cases, the mother is so furious with the father of the child, they don't allow the father to have a relationship with the child. This is so unfair to the child; they will have issues all of their lives behind this foolishness. The child is unable to make the decision for its own life, so it is in the trust and care of more than likely the mother. If the mother is unable to govern her emotions and get over the betrayal, which will take almost a miracle, then the child lives a life of uncertainty. The mother can paint any picture she desires because the child is the recipient of the mother's nurturing. In the child's eyes, the mother is the greatest for being there for him or her, but the reality is, she put a wedge between the child and the father, so the father will always look like the bad guy. For some reason we don't even seek help for the sake of the child but rush into legal battles, as if the child's welfare is the primary reason for the fight, but the reality is, its hurt, pain and sometimes hate; that's the power supply for this fight—not love—for the child's sake. Unfortunately, the child is growing every day and will not stay a child forever. This deception must find a way out. It is easier for the mother to fight the father because of her pain, but she will have more power by forgiving. However, she needs help to do so. Real love from the Greatest Love is what's needed and I'm not talking about numbing the pain, but going for real help from a real source; the source of healing and it can only come from love. Both parents should participate in seeking help, since it took both to make the child. It is worth it for the welfare of the child. Why should a judge have to advocate justice when people are claiming to be godly and good people? We hear it all the time, "I have a good heart!" Really?

No one really knows their heart until that heart has been tested and this situation is just one of the tests of the "heart!" Will they set their pride aside for the innocent life produced by the two? This is a tragedy in our communities throughout this country. Now when we look at our society, we are faced with confused and angry young people, who are expressing themselves through the arts, some through the streets; these have become their platforms. We are hearing the hate and unresolved anger from the confused child within them; it doesn't matter the age. So for every word they don't express to their mother, they shout it out at other women and the world, on social media, in music and in music videos. Who are the songwriters? They are the young adults who are not babies anymore. We may pretend it's for the children, when in fact, we were fighting with our pride and pride is destructive; pride not defused is worse than death. The child grew up believing the lie we set before them because it's easy to manipulate anyone who loves us. The child is now so hurt and confused because they don't want to believe that their mother or father could have been so treacherously selfish! Now without restitution, we have all of these young adults, who are supposed to be our future and become the leaders of our nations. It is scary to think that our future could be left in the hands of the "20's!" The 80 became so damaged, until it was not fit to repair or to reclaim the 100, so selfish was the 80 until we are left with the confused 20! So while we are leaving the family for the 20 that's missing in the relationships, we need to consider the long-term effect it will have on all of us. Now the transgressions of the unfaithful parents are showing themselves through the children.

The lies are being exposed and the truth is coming out through the lyrics of the music and other art forms of expressions. When it comes to freedom of expression and speech, most of our messages are produced by the 20 percent—the twenties (age group) are hurt, incomplete, abandoned, rejected, cover for lies, hidden truths, secrets of the past—those conceived out of brokenness and lust. If they came from an 80/20 situation, which no one will talk about, then this leaves them to be their own therapists. We are too ignorant or proud to admit that we've messed up and need to fix the mistake by seeking professional help, not drugs, alcohol, and not by hiding in religion, but by submitting to the way our Creator God called us to live in the first place. Keep in mind, we all have a real enemy and he's very experienced in the area of destroying families. This may be his Magnum opus to date concerning the present generation. "We can look at the sky and discern the weather, but cannot look at our families and the troubles of the world, and discern, the signs of the times." Listen to our music and its contents; do we hear the cries of the unloved and unwanted children? They are so bound! Hip-hop, especially, has become the most influential, but also lethal. It has become a bittersweet reality for all of us. The youths listen to hip-hop more than their parents and teachers. Its message is becoming destructive where in the beginning it was constructive. It's a tool and instrument to infiltrate the young and hopeful to believe the message of, "Take what you want by any means necessary and live." It started out as the truth but now Satan is using it as a platform to sell more lies and rebellion more so now than in any other generation since the beginning of time and has done the most bittersweet damage.

I'm not claiming to be an expert on anything. I'm not a doctor, or a psychologist. I am but a voice crying out from the horror of drowning in the blood of the innocent, a witness to the damage of an enemy so cunning that he destroys talented and creative people to shed their own blood. This I do know; "I can see!" We are producing lies laced with prosperity and glamor in the form of music videos, causing children to embrace a big lie. When they see videos promoting beautiful houses, exotic cars, designer everything, from clothes to furnishings and harems of women willing to have sex with those with money, why should a man settle for one faithful and committed relationship with anybody? Be a "player!" This is the message infiltrating our nation and ultimately the world and we should know, this would be the annihilation of a people! We cannot build a strong family, community, city, state, nation, and world with a bunch of losers called "players!"

We will not make it; just ask the Devil. He is our reference from "true history." They show women who will work together to please the man with the money and are okay and happy to share their man! We all know a real woman is not okay with sharing her man! See how the lie is so powerful for the hopeless. This lie infuses power to the unfaithful and sets goals to obtain the position of player and male chauvinist! We are not producing a greater percentage of videos to bring good to our world, but evil. Where are the videos to promote education and family; saving the world? Where's the message music of the resolve? Where are the musical prophets? The music geniuses of yesterday used their gifts to bring about awareness to our problems by seeking solutions. Music changed the minds of a people and the world! The music greats who are still here on this earth must be in torment to see how the greatness, influence, and power of music has been polluted and is being used to destroy our world. It was good for some of them to go on home and not witness such evil. To those who make music selling lies, sending children to hell, I don't believe it's that simple; God has to judge every case. When a child between the ages of 11 to 19 is made to believe through media, that they can obtain luxurious lifestyles by being vicious and evil, something is terribly twisted about those who make a living off of such "destructive deception." What's sad is the dope, cars, jewelry, houses, and clothes were not purchased from a gangster lifestyle at all. These dudes are living in Hollywood and similar communities waiting on a legitimate paycheck from their record companies who they work for; these are all lies! They do not feel you, they do not speak for you, and they are not you who are struggling! They are promoters for the destruction of our youth while going to more funerals and having prisons built. It has become a great business of death and destruction—what lies! We have seen more deaths than have ever occurred in our previous historical wars. We worry about wars or even a possible civil war; well look around—it's already here! Young people are out on the streets trying to come up on the destruction of their own people because they've made these artists their heroes and the message is to sell dope, be a gangster, a pimp, a liar, a deceiver, a player, a whore, and a murderer. Surely, this is the way to prosperity, right?

Do we see or are we so blind to how hypocritical we are? We are, after all, the same people with children trying to give them a good life. Wait a minute! Your victims are dying in the streets of the "hood" all around the world because there are ghettos everywhere while you are sending your children to the best schools and living the best lives. Something is sick about this! Your "message music" caused a child to kill someone and he's gone to prison or will be executed. One mother is in the courtroom crying while the other is at the graveyard burying her child and you feel like you're on top of the game for destroying life. We need to fix this! We need to turn back to God for real! We have too many churches, religions, and religious leaders idly standing by or hiding behind closed doors preaching. But true ministry is serving, not being served.

How should God judge this? Because He will. It's His job to do so, but we have only one lifetime to build our case. I pray for the woman because she is usually the 100 percent turned 80 percent, losing the man who was looking for his 20. By doing so the woman is now trying to be like him and ultimately producing the negative, the loss, the destructive, the murderer, the players, the pimp, the gangster, the liar, the whore...need I say more...I'm tired. I cannot go on with the rest! Some women have left a good home and marriage because she thinks she is missing something. She wants to have good time; she has left 80 percent looking for the 100 percent and found her 20 percent. Not only did she find her 20, but this will become repetitively ridiculous, to get 20 after 20 and after 20, now her children have witnessed the mother being played and they will more than likely have issues with men; they will get their share of 20's also. After Mom and Dad showed them that marriage has no value, then why should they enter into an agreement that they won't keep? We have become the greatest "covenant breakers!" on this planet! We don't keep our word even after we put together this big ceremony as if it's the wedding that makes the marriage, but the ceremony should be a parallel of a celebrated union of a lifetime commitment and the joy of family. We even go into church and stand before God, the preacher, witnesses and family and exchange vows, only to break them as if it's a joke! God is a joke? Maybe we think so; that's why we continue more and more to remove Him from our lives, our laws, our government, our conscience, and just as sure we are born to die, the day will come when He will remove many of us from His. We have too many divorces from those of us who vowed to love each other and be committed until death takes us apart. The truth is; some men and women are no good and selfish. The woman has so much power and influence. Will she take note of how misguided that is? Look at history! Whatever it took to get your man, continue in it to keep your man. Make a conscious decision to make babies by "love and making love" not random, lustful, hot sex! At least we need to be responsible when a child is born irresponsibly by lust or entrapment.

It is so unfair to the baby because the baby is born with a job. The baby should be loved and celebrated, not find themselves in a pool of stress and mess! When a wife holds out on her husband for sex, she is using witchcraft. You don't want your husband cheating, but you ration out sex and love to him as if he's on welfare for love! Please, we need to stop playing games! The woman must understand who hates her! I am thoroughly convinced of this. Beware of the deceptions of your enemy. A woman who's married, hanging out in a club with girlfriends who are single, is as wicked as a man who's married hanging out in a whorehouse taking a nap before going home after work. We cannot play with fire and not get burned! We need to tell the truth of how many families and relationships have been destroyed for a fake out time on the town with losers and this goes for the man and the woman. We need to share our stories and tell people the truth of how it played out and ultimately ended! While we are going through this foolishness, on the other side of the world, war is going on and building up more and more intensely! We cannot go on much longer without paying the penalties for the disrespect we are giving to the King! True kings are born by natural account. They count up the costs with enemies and allies. They are wise to know whose side they are on before they dispatch armies for war. Once unleashed, there's no turning back until His enemy is annihilated! We have this mess because somebody left looking for their 20. God gave Lucifer everything and He went looking for his 20. Satan is looking for his 20, the Devil is looking his 20, the man is looking for his 20, the woman Is looking for her 20, and the children of this generation are off the meter in anger, because they are the generation of the "20's."

Heaven has released a vial on this generation for all to see; it will be called, the "20/20" generation! A double portion; perfect vision! Open your eyes and see the transgressions long awaited for the heavens to see through this generation! By the year 2020 the face of our nation will have changed forever! When a woman has a "man's heart," it is hard for him to walk away or let go. Women need to understand this and stop giving a man your body and all of your goods without knowing him or having a commitment, if that's what you're looking for. If marriage is not what you're looking for, but a relationship, then at least make him court you for 120 days before you even consider giving him sex. This is the relationship's "evaluation period." This will give you guys a chance to date and get to know each other on a real note. This will allow time to deal with normal life occurrences such as work, being at home, chill time, and you get to see how the person handles day-to-day life, whatever that may bring. If that man has to give you excuses every holiday or have some kind of emergency to where he's not able to be with you, then he's married or in a committed relationship... and it's not you! Too many women "give it up" too fast and blow the opportunity to know what the devil the man is. You gave your "cookies and milk"" and he's having the whole meal with trimmings at his real home with the lady of his life.

Sad to say, he's in love with her but she has gotten too comfortable in the relationship and perhaps arrogant enough to think, "He'll never step out on this good thing!" She may be right about the good thing but it's not that good if he's not getting it on a regular basis. When it comes to a man, he will find a substitute for what's missing. Some would even indulge in internet babes, thinking it's better than cheating and they may not see it as "cheating." Nonetheless, he's searching for that missing "20 percent." "Be wise as serpents but harmless as doves, ladies!" Monitor your relationships and stop being lazy! Stop shopping to look good. Stop giving up the goods in your own marriage; this is fake, shade! Most women will argue the fact and I quote, "I'm not doing this for no one but me!" So she wants her husband to believe that she is going through all of that trouble for herself and nobody else? If that's true, then run! This only means she is the most selfish person on the planet! No matter what you do or give her, it will never be enough! Lust for things can never be satisfied, so go and find love. This is the spirit of Lucifer! She can't love you or anyone else, there's no room, because she's too in love with herself! She cannot see beyond her own lust fulfilling desires. These women are good at catching men, they are great seducers, but not good at keeping a man! This is deception. She knows well in advance that she cannot keep up with that act for one man; she will bore very easily with you. In fact, most of these women are the "20's." But mostly, these women do not want to be alone. In most cases, the man gets caught up in how good she looks; well this is an investment.

The new guy does not know that everything she is or has, she has gotten them from a collection of men; previous fake relationships! Her wardrobe extends over years of men she's been with; they are gifts as rewards for her service, but you better not call her a whore or prostitute, she thinks she has to work a corner to qualify! What's even more amazingly disgraceful is that most women who are living this way have children! She will be good at seducing you, probably the best you've ever had, but it's part of the game. Her teacher is the serpent, who's her enemy, and she doesn't even know him. She uses all of her men and dates to accumulate gifts. One gets her perfume, the other a blouse, another shoes, another a dress, another the salon bill, another the car payment and it goes on and on. All of them will pay for her to eat at some restaurant; she's a junkie when it comes to that. This is where you get sized up—on the dinner date. She will usually order more than she can eat to take some home. Like a junkie, she is always taking something from her date home! All of her dates need to have a good hustle going on because she uses them to buy her something as often as possible and pretends to be most grateful and thankful! They are financing her looks and appearance. This is to make her look good, to enable her to capture her next victim (date). Most women have no clue that the same serpent that abused her growing up is the same spirit using her to commit these acts. She will be cleaned and polished, just in case she comes across that someone who she thinks is worth the risk of losing her relationship if she's currently in one. She will get her hair done, paint her nails, and wear that special outfit to test it on the guys and women!

She usually goes shopping even if she's not buying anything; this is how she prowls and tests the prowler. Women love attention, this is how she's wired. It is not to take away from a lady; we're simply exposing the destroyer! They will wear exotic underwear as well, and again, this is just in case if she plans to go all the way; she wants to be fresh, clean, exotic, and sexy! This is another problem you will have; her previous dates will always pop up and snarl because they want her to freak them and they will indirectly test you to see if you are a new piece or trying to be serious. If they think you are serious, they will make an attempt to disrespect you because they have no respect for her. They know what she is and when she was through with them, she cut off the sex with them too. But there is something about seeing her with another man; the man wants to hit it again and most likely she will be turned on too. If she is she will hook up with him one more time when you're not around. They will have a little signal; trust and believe her phone is locked. She can't explain why she is this way; she just knows she's trying to live!

This may sound a little "crass" or, as they say in Europe, "a little cheeky," but it's time to expose the "real enemy" and it's not her. She needs to see how the serpent is using her to destroy the family. Stay away from that tree! As long as these games are being played, another boy turned man is calling you "a hoe!" It used to be a time where you had the girls you could take home to mama and the ones you couldn't, but today, they're all mixed up and rolling together. It is so unfair for all women to be labeled as "hoes!"

Listen to what the young men of this generation are saying. They have no respect for women, especially black women. Why is the world so comfortable calling any woman out of her name? What happened to the love in songs? They have become strictly "lust" songs. Lust doesn't love anybody. Lust is selfish and can never be satisfied, no matter how much you give to it. Love should look for love and lust should do the same and look for lust. If he doesn't love you then he will lust you and inevitably leave you. If you are looking for love, then look where love is and that is in the heart.

We need to fix this mess!

We need to face reality! These young men are seeing this and putting it out there! We have leaders who have hidden away from the truth for so long, that it has blown up in our faces; we ought to be ashamed! This should be a reality check for all of us! If this is the perception of our women today, then who would be confident or want to get married, when they feel that the woman can't be trusted. Did you hear him say, "Her ringer for her phone was off and her wedding ring was off of her hand while she was seducing him?" This is real. So why would men of power and riches want one woman when she can't be trusted? Seeing how many married women are in the clubs, the streets, and social media, on jobs looking for a supplier! This usually happens after she has you.

All the passion will diminish; it's just a matter of time. While you're working to take care of her, she's on the prowl for the most attention from the next guy who looks like he can do her better than you. In my experience, I've never met a woman who defends herself in this manner to remain faithful. She was hungry for attention and one day someone approached her that was too tempting to let go by. She sowed her seeds and now it's harvest time; another marriage gone to hell because of the lie. So my advice is don't play with fire because you will get burned! The person does not cheat when they get physical but when they did it in their heart... it was already done; it's just a matter of time. No matter how much you give to lust, it will always want more. No matter how great the relationship appears to be from an adulteress situation, it has never been a success to even talk about. The chances of infidelity as the foundation for a loving, long-term relationship, is slim to none. If he or she loves you today, hold on, because that won't be true tomorrow. Once one of the two commits infidelity, breaking the other party's heart, you will have your share of heart breaks. They will be manifested eventually. You will have many sleepless nights because the lack of trust in each other. Even when moving on to another relationship, you will not be able to leave the baggage behind. You will constantly remember the lies and deceit you were treacherous enough to pull off to pull the wool over your partner's eyes.

You will never trust each other because you both know "the devil is a liar" and both of you are liars and living a lie! All of us who have lived long enough know "a lie cannot stand!" Now what started out as a good time has turned into torment for your minds and soul! We have too many religions for this to happen right before our eyes and in our homes, and sometimes, in church! What? The 80/20 rule is not biased or prejudiced. We do not work together to make 100, but we only can exist when 100 splits or becomes distracted and lacks vigilance. We're only here because you have had some of the most prestigious guests to ever walk this planet; from kings to queens, politicians to priests, law enforcement to prisoners, husbands and wives, from the church-house to the whorehouse, even the courthouse. We do not discern between situations; neither do we have regard for circumstances. All we know is that we must accommodate and we'll see where it goes. But I will let you in on a little secret; you will feel good in the beginning if you can overcome your guilt, shame, and condemnation. We will take care of you for as long as you need us to, but we cannot guarantee that you'll ever recover from what we will do to you. Your wife or husband may not want you back or see you the same way again but you will have a good time with us for a little while; then justice will prevail "80/20!" I'm a believer and I challenge all who love God and are tired of standing by, watching a generation self-destruct, to come together for the saving of a people.

Let's put our differences aside for goodness's sake! God is watching! We need to come to together for the common good. All it takes is courage and agreement. The leaders in times before us would not idly stand by and allow this to happen. Look at what has happened to us in just the past 60 years. Where do we go from here? Where will we end up in the next 60 years as a people and a nation? What will happen to our women?

It should make us wonder; who's the real enemy? Who is hating? But I decided to speak for myself, just to let you know. Although you didn't love me, you never loved me, but you gave me my names; freak, freaky, rejected, satisfying, revengeful, sexy, pleasure, a piece, hoe, trick, hooker, chicken head, no good, good for nothing, hoochie mama, gold digger, faithfully unfaithful, seductive, bitch, fling, and thing.

How long can we continue like this as a people, as a nation? Someone is responsible for me, says your "20!"

XIII

❦

Chapter 13: The New Babylon

The Bible prophetically speaks of this change in something called, "The New Babylon." This is a nation, but more so a "system" similar to "Ancient Babylon" to bring about a global change! Probably no one would volunteer for this change but because of a series of catastrophic events over the past, change is welcomed on a desperate level at this point. We are looking everywhere and to almost anyone.

Ancient Babylon was on the site of modern-day Iraq. King Nebuchadnezzar was ruler and the superpower of the world at his time. Saddam Hussein believed he was chosen and purposed as the leader to resurrect Ancient Babylon. His goal was to show the world the New Babylon and therefore fulfill the prophecy of Babylon's rise to its former state of global power. Hussein was well on his way to being the modern-day Nebuchadnezzar. Nebuchadnezzar was humbled by the Almighty God at one point and lost his mind leaving his crown and throne, living like an animal in the forest for seven years. As mysteriously as he left his kingdom, one day he returned and gave his testimony that the true king is the one who lives forever and the Almighty God was indeed the King of Kings.

There was no nation or king greater than him on the earth and all kings and nations feared him. During this era, King Nebuchadnezzar subdued Jerusalem and the Israelite people, enslaving those who survived. Babylon had many people of different races and languages and the Israelite people were no exception. The Israelites were slaves in Babylon for about seventy years during this time. Just as it is and was for any nation, the slaves brought Babylon unprecedented wealth and power. Nebuchadnezzar did the unthinkable and subdued the Capital, which was Jerusalem. He desecrated the temple and took all of the riches and valuables found inside, taking all the sacred things including the most valued of all, (at least to the Israelite People) "the Ark of the Covenant." This daring and bold action of disregard to God and man demanded the attention and respect of every nation and king, making Nebuchadnezzar the most ruthless and fearless of all kings. This put Babylon ahead of all nations and kingdoms. All nations now were looking to Babylon for trade and business opportunities in hopes of obtaining wealth and prosperity. Nebuchadnezzar had a vision and the newly founded free labor would help bring it to pass. He desired to make history and be the greatest king in the world. With the slaves under his authority, he had more than enough resources to bring his vision to fruition.

Slaves in any nation or society are one of the greatest commodities and make the nation wealthy. With Nebuchadnez-zar's arrogance, power, army, and vision, there was no king or nation that could come close to his greatness, earning his kingdom the acclaim as "Babylon the Great!" King Nebuchad-nezzar viewed himself as a god and the greatest ruler ever. He changed the game while having the world in the palm of his hands. He was not concerned with anyone's love for him but thrived on power and everyone fearing him. He literally built an image of himself demanding for everyone to bow down and worship him. He didn't have the support of his people, he had their worship. Sometimes we think we are supporting when in fact it is worship. Worship is giving your all to honor, regard, and devote to a cause or person, no matter what.

God put this man in power to expose the true hearts of His people, especially those who claim to believe in God and serve Him. Whoever you worship you would definitely serve them in whatever capacity. Question, who were they truly worshiping or what? They would say God but they worshiped gold, money, and material things. So God gave them a king who understood wealth and exposed their true hearts. God used a gentile king to show the world how much the priest and preachers loved money, so he gave them an image of what they really worshiped. The king would have made an im-age about one hundred feet tall and approximately twenty-five feet wide of the finest gold. If you complied, you would receive his favor but if not you would consequently receive his judgment. He executed the King of Israel's general and the King's sons right before his eyes. Then he made him a slave. He was sure to mention to him of the Prophet Jeremiah and the word God had given him although Nebuchadnezzar was not a server of this God of those people. But he made it clear that their God delivered them into his hands. He also killed the false prophets who caused the people to rebel against God. Nebuchadnezzar knew if these people really would have been faithful and loyal to their God he would not have been given the authority to seize them and capture them in battle. For a long time, Israel had forgotten how God had delivered them from many enemies and plots to overthrow them. THEY WERE SO BLESSED THEY THOUGHT THEY WERE UNTOUCHABLE. They did not understand it was God who set it in the hearts to do His Will. God extended His grace but they would not turn from their lewdness.

The Prophet Jeremiah gave the king messages repeatedly of what was going to come. God had placed His words in Jeremiah's mouth. Jeremiah was God's witness and messenger to warn the king and people of their religious apostasy under Manasseh. Josiah worked on religious reform and Jeremiah supported it with enthusiasm until he realized that it was not changing the people's hearts. It would be a couple of years after Josiah's death, when the Battle of Carchemish established Babylon's control over western Asia (605 BC). From that time Jeremiah advocated submission to Babylon, but without success.

Jeremiah's ministry was over forty years. The nation was in a mess when he was born and his own father was a priest and had been for many of the years of apostasy over the period of four kings. Twenty-one years of religious apostasy and political weakness made the fall of Jerusalem in 586 B.C., and exile, inevitable. Jeremiah Chapter 23 is where you hear how he was a warrior for God, warning the religious leaders first to stop the idolatry and return back to God. The pastors were fleecing the sheep and God's people were in trouble. The leaders were so vain they did whatever they could to get prosperity. The pastors and prophets had become obvious liars for their own selfish gain. The distressing circumstances in which Jeremiah worked, and the extraordinary extent to which idolatry had replaced revealed religion in Judah, are clearly mirrored in Jeremiah's prophecies. So also is Jeremiah's spiritual anguish occasioned by this apostasy yet he is no pessimist. He's God's warrior, witness, and watchman. When reading his writings, you can clearly see his lifelong mission to get the people back in alignment with God. Jeremiah brought awareness of the treacheries against God but no one was listening.

They misunderstood the material things for God's blessings and approval for their lifestyles. In the meantime, Jeremiah was bringing a message of God, wanting a divorce from Judah. The prophets who had a political stake with the people saw Jeremiah as a threat to their imaginary future because it would never be a reality. But of course the false prophets and messengers had the ears of the king and powers that be. They plotted again and again to silence the truth, and one particular revelation was to throw the messenger into prison. In Jeremiah's oracles, God the moral governor of the world is Israel's covenant God. Through Israel He sought to achieve moral purposes. Alas, the northern kingdom adulteries with Baalim compelled to divorce her (that is, exile) her. Judah, the southern kingdom, failed to learn from Israel's experience. She outdid Israel in sexual impurities, yet Judah repudiated the charges of religious infidelity. Therefore, God must judge her.

"And the Lord said unto me, the backsliding Israel hath justified herself more than treacherous Judah." (Jeremiah 3:11)

Repentance might have stayed divorce proceedings (exile), her adulteries notwithstanding, so great is the Lord's grace. But so established was Judah in lewdness that she was incapable of moral amendment. Gradually, social virtues disappeared. Going to church, talking to God, sacrifices, and ritual failed as substitutes for repentance and righteousness. Judah's appalling sinfulness meant that sin must be congenital, hence, her moral inability. It sprang from a sinful nature. Judgment was inescapable, and exile. But exile is not the final word.

Nebuchadnezzar took Jehoiakim's son, Jehoiachin, who reigned in his father's stead. He also did evil in the Lord's sight, according to all that his father had done. Nebuchadnezzar came up against Jerusalem and besieged the city. Jehoiachin, King of Judah, was taken to the king of Babylon—he, his mother, his servants, his princes, and his officers. The king of Babylon took him in the eighth year of his reign. The King of Babylon took all treasures of the king's house, and cut in pieces all the vessels of gold, which King Solomon of Israel had made in the temple of the Lord, as the Lord commanded him. He carried away all Jerusalem, and all the princes and all the mighty men of valor, the strong and ready for war, and all the skilled labor, builders, metal workers, and the craftsmen. He took all but left the poorest of people of the land behind. He took captive the king's mother, the king's wives, his officers, and the mighty men of the land.

The King of Babylon made Mattaniah, Jehoiachin's uncle,

king in his place and changed his name to Zedekiah. Zedekiah was twenty-one years old when he began to reign. He reigned eleven years in Jerusalem. He also did evil in the sight of the Lord, according to all that Jehoiakim had done. Now this was the fourth king under the warnings of the Prophet Jeremiah. Jeremiah's message had been consistent for almost forty years and not one king had listened or even warned the people of the destruction to come if they did not turn away from evil. Jeremiah told all of them to repent and return to good and refrain from evil and immoral doings. Instead they silenced the messenger. Because of these evil leaders, God gave power to their enemies to put them out of their own city, to make them slaves, to remind them of how He was the one to deliver them as a people after over four hundred years of bondage and mistreatment from the Pharaoh and Egypt. God used Moses as His messenger to the King of Egypt and he would not reason or take heed to the warning. So here we go again. Why not learn from history? For some reason they thought they would skip the history lesson. The purpose of the Passover in the first month of the year on the 14th day to the 21st day, seven days of unleavened bread to remind them of when they were slaves and how He set them free; no one had mercy on them but God. Now these are the descendants of former slaves being taken into bondage again as a people. The travesty is they heard the stories of their ancestors being slaves but never experienced bondage themselves. Their stubbornness and pride have them caught like prey in a net. What is their fate?

Supposedly, being a God-fearing and serving nation meant being a multicultural place of business, trade, commerce, and wealth built on free labor—slaves who are strong, smart, and intellectually gifted; the sorted out talents of all races. No mistakes were made in knowing that the Israelites are the slaves in this nation—everyone knows this. There were selected and favored slaves to represent the wisdom of the king, and although not recognized by society as a whole, those who were in the king's circle knew these slaves had divine favor and knowledge that could not be denied.

The slaves were full of knowledge in science, math, and astrology, interpreting visions and dreams. Nebuchadnezzar's grandson, Darius, is now king and makes a conscious decision to bring restoration to the slaves and ultimately gives them back their land, opportunities, and even temples. Of course, there are Babylonian descendants of Nebuchadnezzar's order and have benefited from the ways of dealing with slaves and wealth. They felt threatened by the restoration of the slaves back to their own land and freedom. The fear of these leaders of Babylon caused them to sabotage the Israelite people, although against the king's wishes and even law. The Babylonian leaders' desperation to remain in power caused them to violate lives and laws to keep the Israelites under their feet. Those who were in control of the Babylonian government and laws were even falsifying documents submitted to the government on behalf of the Israelite people. As a result of these government officials' sabotaging tactics, the work of the Israelites was hindered and ultimately came to a stop. They made the Israelite people appear melancholy and lazy, causing the king despair. The people had petitioned the king for years for their desire to have their own land, and to build/restore their temple. The king was confused after receiving false reports as to why the Israelites stopped work on projects in their own community, because their actions were a contradiction to their much anticipated request to build their temple enabling them to worship their own God. King Darius discovered that the leaders who were in charge of these operations were at the very core of the problems. They violated the king's orders and laws of the land by sabotaging these people. The king made a new order for the Israelite people to resume building their temple and community. The king's new law and order stated: anyone hindering the Israelite people from building and prospering will answer directly to the king.

In whatever way you hindered them, the king would hinder you. If you tore down their walls, the walls of your house would be torn down. If you pulled down any planks from their ceilings and roofs, the same would be done to your houses. If you mistreated or abused them in anyway, then you would be mistreated and abused. If you harmed or killed any of the Israelite people, then you and your family would be killed. Then the king financed the building cost of the Israelite people because of the actions of his leaders sabotaging them. He gave them all the support they needed to complete their work and told them to build with Godspeed because their work had been hindered for two years. This was the king's wisdom to restore a people who had been wrongfully treated, torn down, and hindered from progressing. The king understood as most Babylonians at that time, the Israelites had their own land and possessions before they were made slaves and were very instrumental in the prosperity and wealth of "Babylon the Great" as the Babylonians' now knew and experienced greatness provided by the skills, minds, and innovations of a slaved people. Simply put, if the Israelite people could build and prosper the Babylonians then why could they not prosper themselves if just given the same opportunities without hindering or tampering with them and their work? Ancient Babylon is now called Iraq and New Babylon is not in the east but in the west as the United States of America. Babylon is not about the geographical location, but it is a system, demanding a dominate mindset over the inferior or made-to-be degenerate people. North America is the "New Babylon" talked about over 2,000 years ago when the east had no knowledge of her. The prophecies of slavery, slave trade, the borders of Africa, Ethiopia, even the ships are described, the captains and the dead who were thrown overboard in the sea (ocean). It clearly speaks well in advance of the brutality, murder, and building of cities on innocent blood. Her sins have come up to heaven and the Elders ask, "How long before her judgment?" This nation's fate will hinge on the glory, power, and authority of the woman who understands that her position and posture is the only relevance and resolve in the one having 20/20 divine vision, an eye-opening being such as herself, because she has suffered from the beginning of time. It is inevitable that the Woman will be the Super Power of this New Age! 2020 was the year of corrective vision. God divinely showed us how much we had.

New Babylon is and will continue to be the instrument used to expose the Anti-Christ, his intent, and spirit. He will come after her, not to unite but to control. He will not be able to resist showing himself in these times as he could not resist showing himself to Eve in the Garden. Once the woman is in position as the most powerful being on this planet, then we will witness unprecedented change because she will be given glory and power as the world has never seen! Food for thought: don't look for her to be righteous so much as her being smart and powerful. Like it or not, she will be justified, because everything must come to an end. For her long time haters this is her awaited time and season. Her destiny is inevitable and connected to her beginning trials and many tribulations over the ages. Considered second class, she is moved to the head position and the entire world will see her! Revelation 18 cannot be fulfilled until she sits on the throne. She will have Power and Glory that the world has never seen or witnessed until now!

She is like no other woman in the world. She is uniquely made of not one race but many races. She is every race and creed. She learned religion and through it built a uniquely intimate relationship with her God. She is multicultural. She has in her the languages of all the world. She is the face of the ancient and modern world all in one. Her shape is perfectly designed to wear the most beautiful garments money can buy.

She knows how to entertain. She is humility and majesty alike. She knows war and peace. She is the most talented in the entire world. The producer of the greatest skills, gifts, and talents sought after throughout the entire world. Many desire to be like her and to get to know her. They want to live with you, be like you, and are willing to leave their own land to live with you in your land in hopes of one day being accepted as a citizen. She is so powerful but so nurturing. She's highly educated and yet represents those that may never get a great education. She is willing to help others. Though known for her beauty she's also known for her democracy, getting her hands dirty, and the tenacity to start from nothing with not enough reservation to not make her journey. She's like a person running for her life. She left her own land to start a new life. She loves liberty and freedom. She left her home and sought after the freedom. The freedom to live a beautiful life without fear or made to be in any religion against her will. She began a relationship with the Almighty God.

Looking back over her life, she was abused. She was limited in her achievements because of being a woman. She learned about her God and began to worship Him not just as religion but as a relationship. Through her relationship she overcame all fears and obstacles. She knows what it is to be homeless and lonely, unable to return home without losing her dignity. She suffered sickness and disease. It was thought that she would fail, returning back where she came from with shame. But against all odds, she stayed her course. She is made of a new land not knowing her own address. She didn't even know what to call herself. She suffered an identity crisis. God protected her against war and disease, although these things were inevitable, God gave her favor. She had favor with God and men. She learned how to live through her struggles understanding with God all things are possible. She found help in her new place to live. What should we do for those who have helped us that don't look like us? They are friendly and helpful. We look different on the outside, but somehow, we seem to be the same. From the grassroots of this new land she's able to survive.

With so many challenges she learns how to pray for herself. Some days she feels lonely for home; the only place she ever knew. Missing the traditions of home and family, she was challenged to embark upon her own traditions from her experiences. She was missing the look of cathedrals and temples, places of worship, having no priest in this new and unknown world, and having the foundation laid in her from her homeland; this is so different. She is challenged with having to connect with the God within her. She's learning a new strength about herself. If God is with me I will succeed. Having the freedom to worship God without any influence whatsoever, this was her chance to know God for herself. This was the beginning of a new nation but is somehow in conversations described as a woman. Because every gift and attribute of the woman will be needed to make this thing happen.

Without her skills we will have no other recourse than to return back to Europe. Life is dependent on the woman to give birth, the very life in a new place called, "The New World," coming from Europe and representing the Queen more than any other being of power in the world. Women have seen their share of abuse and struggles of women of power in the European Dynasties through the rise and fall of many kings and leaders, using women to do miracles when all else failed, and having women to pray for change only to deny her a promotion when said change arrives. She must be silent and grateful when things are going good but is called upon when all hell breaks loose. Somehow when she is called upon, she never fails; the threat dissipates. Maybe in this new world the woman could be forgiven of the burden from the Garden of Eden and of Eve (The Mother of all Living).

Could it be possible in this brand new start that she will be respected for her hard work and contributions to this great endeavor? Here we go again—new place same stuff. She's now faced with outbreaks, disease, disputes, war, rape, and abuse at home and afar. Where does the strength come from except she knows somehow it's greater than herself? How is it that when troubles come she is depended on for survival but when things turn around she must be silent? She is the voice in private that wins wars in public. How is this new world treating her the same way as the old world? She did not come here for this. Something must change. The more this New World is getting a face and place in society the slimmer her chances are to be heard, not just seen. Why is it that I am shown to the entire world as beautiful but have no voice? "Seen but not heard" is someone's plan for her and she is paining to be heard. She knows that is her voice and counsel in private that brings about victory and resolve publicly. It is her and the God in her that guides through trouble. She is constantly being used but not openly respected. Desperate, some have turned to evil after feeling trapped. Where is her respect in the process of decisions?

The book of Revelation speaks concerning Lucifer, Satan, and Jezebel for the end times. The false Prophet (preacher, teacher, pastor, and leader) is very important to these three in the last days because their job is to deceive through religion and politics. Jezebel can never be satisfied no matter how much you give her or do for her...it's never enough neither can be. She is a consumer who started out as a producer, driven by greed, never need. Jezebel is described as the spirit that is the driving force of a nation to be used by the Antichrist to set up his kingdom on earth. Jezebel started out as a wife and became a whore, but not with men. She never cheated on her husband with her body, but in her mind, with vanity and material things, she was always having an affair with money...

this is called, "Whoredom." This is the worst kind of whore because she's blind to her state and thinks of herself as successful. While she was buying one thing her mind was already on buying another, while receiving a gift from one person, she was already thinking on who else was going to bless her or bring her another gift.

This had become her normal way of life—never satisfied and always chasing things! She was so deceived, she thought this was the way people should live. But the problem was, she was absorbed with herself. She did not want anyone in her circle to do anything but worship her, and serve her and her desires. She is the most selfish and self-centered of all beings! She will kill everyone's dreams to sustain her own; she will also sabotage you while pretending to be your greatest supporter and adviser. When you look around, you will see, Jezebel is and has always been the "Cancer" to your Destiny! The nation who served (THE) God, but now serves many gods, is that nation...the whore described in Revelation chapter 18. The spirit of Jezebel will be very instrumental in fulfilling this prophecy. "She is a queen and is no widow and will see no sorrow, so from the wealth of slavery, injustice and innocent blood!" The blood is crying out to God asking how long before they will be avenged. No matter the fantasy, the slaves will not be given power to avenge themselves, lest they be judged with her, because now the slaves with their freedom has become just as wicked as the masters of olden times. Who is our father? That is the question. We will seek to please our father, whoever that might be. Our actions are a pledge to him; because the book of Revelation calls her, "Beautiful."

God will have a woman in the seat as "CEO" of that nation before destruction hits as to honor Him.

She is called, "Mystery Babylon the Great!" For in one hour your judgment has come. One hour in God's time is "60 years." From 1968 to now 2021, God has been waiting on an apology. We have seven more years before our hour is up!

The New Babylon is Babylon the Great—the city that sits upon may waters.

XIV

❦

Chapter 14: America the Beautiful

This Woman will be the Greatest Ruler ever seen in our modern world! Her Greatness will be the Glory of God not seen for many centuries! The more she trusts God in her decisions, the more power she will be given. Her obedience to Him is the key to her historical success and unprecedented achievements! This will come with a price—other's jealousy—but no one will be able to touch her or bring her harm because the Earth will help her; God will command them to do so! The favor and wisdom of God is with her. He will come to her in dreams and visions. She already has part of the vision right now! She can't quite explain it, but she knows that she has been chosen by the heavens and the God of the Universe to take this assignment. She has been prepared from her very existence for this moment in time, orchestrated by Eternity. Every test she was given was monitored and graded for the crown. She will be honored as the greats of days of old.

We, today, are not a culture of kings and queens, but it will be such a reverence for this woman because she will have answers and solutions that no leader has had since olden biblical history. She will have the greatest achievements to date. The world will cooperate with her by orders from God Almighty. God has equipped her with everything she needs right at her fingertips. She is not easily moved or foolishly persuaded. She knows who she is and whose she is. She's not the public figure of religion because she's kingdom-minded and has a personal relationship with God. When she was hit with troubles that should have sent her plunging to her demise, she dismissed counsel from men and women (very wise counsel) and chose her Counselor to have the final say—and He did! When she obeyed God in this situation, it was the beginning of wisdom for her like a female version of King Solomon! Her wisdom is a badge of honor.

She is the chosen vessel of the greatest prophecy to ever be fulfilled. We cannot do this without her. She is not biased or prejudiced, but just. She is for all races around the world, but very focused and wise at home. Lucifer and his alter-ego, Satan, are working on recruiting a woman for their achievements to becoming the deadliest of all living beings! This is why we must be aware of this transition! "There's nothing new under the sun." Lucifer is the master of fallen angels while Satan is the master of demon spirits. Both of these spirits operate in pride, hate, and rebellion against God! Lucifer is a master deceiver, and he's very charismatic. Satan is very blunt, egotistic, and cares not about what you think of him. He's selfish and determined to win. Neither Lucifer nor Satan have the gift of repentance—they are never wrong and apologetic;

it's not in their nature. The sign of one operating in this spirit is that they will not repent or turn from their evil—they lack the ability to do so. They will never take responsibility for any wrongdoing or want to apologize for anything. They have too much pride to do this. No matter how many lives they destroy, they will always have a justification. Lucifer proved to God while in heaven where his loyalty was and still is—in the riches, power, titles and position. He cared not about God—only God's stuff.

This is the reason for Jesus coming in the form that he did. The Temple was full of God's enemies posing to be priests who loved the Lord. God came in poverty to test the hearts of all humanity. Imagine having all power, and being the Creator of all things and life. Of all things God chooses to come as a poor craftsman. He was the first "Undercover Boss!" If the world would have known who he was they would have pretended to care for him and his mission. Imagine how many gold diggers would have sucked up to Him? Look at how the Priest in God's temple hated Him. They knew they were in it for the money, not the people. Jesus really cared for the people and this made them look bad. They purposely plotted to have him executed. For all the people falsely accused by "the powers that be" for whatever reason, The SON OF GOD GOT YOU. THERE IS NO REST IN PEACE! Lucifer spun that lie. You can't raise hell and then go somewhere and rest forever. Jesus said to His perpetrators, "You will see me at the right hand of the power of God. You will see Abraham, Isaac, and Jacob but will not sit at the table with them, but will be cast into eternal darkness and damnation. There will be wailing and gnashing of teeth."

Think about it if Jesus (Yashua) is not the Son of God then who was He? This man did not come into this world flexing His power and wealth. He basically hid out understanding the common people and their everyday struggles. When He started His Ministry He was able to relate to us (our humanity). How could a man who was falsely accused by (religious leaders) the Pharisees, convicted and executed for many crimes, and handed over to the Romans to carry out the order? At this time, Israel wasn't a self-governing nation, so they could not carry out the order themselves. In turn they would ultimately manipulate the government to kill Him. The very last time Jesus was at the temple, He prophesied to them before His arrest saying, "You will not see me again until you learn to cry blessed is he who comes in the name of the Lord, this temple shall be destroyed and not one stone will stand upon the other." About 50 AD Jerusalem was under siege and the temple was destroyed. Not only this, but later the Roman Government changed time as we know it. They started time over in honor of this man who had chosen 12 men to be His followers under the reign and rule of these two emperors: Julius Caesar and Augustus Caesar. During Jesus's days on earth 10 months made up our calendar year and every 3 1/2 to 5 years the calendar would have to be adjusted to meet with the sun and moon. These men who were feared by most of the known world used their power to change the world forever. They set the calendars by adding 2 more months to it, "July (Julius) and August (Augustus). Everything before Jesus will be B.C. (Before Christ) and everything after Him will be called A.D. (*Anno Domini*, which is Latin for "in the year of the Lord"). Why would these two men of the world's greatest power, considered by the Hebrew or Israelite people (Jews) to be infidels or Gentiles, use their time to rule to start time over in honor of a Jew? Why would Europeans give such a monumental historic moment in time to honor this poor man? Why not leave themselves this legacy and honor for Roman history of accomplishments? Remember when our calendars read, "1968 In the Year of Our Lord"?

There's only ONE explanation, Jesus in fact was and is the true Son of God who came to this world to finish His work and save His people. His blood was needed to complete the serum—to separate good from evil, love from hate, the truth from the lie, life from death, and find the cure to heaven's greatest outbreak and pandemic, which was "SIN!"

This same Jesus who rose from the dead visited His Disciple-Apostle John on the Island of Patmos and showed him of the future. The Book of Revelation was showed to John and he was instructed to write what he saw—not to analyze, but to just write. In this same book is where we find the coming of the judgment of the great whore who sits on many waters. How she is able to seduce the entire world and commits fornication with the kings (powerful leaders). Those of the earth are drunk from her Kool-Aid.

Upon her head was written, "MYSTERY BABYLON THE GREAT MOTHER OF HARLOTS AND ABOMINATIONS OF THE EARTH."

I saw the woman, drunk with the blood of the saints and with the blood of the martyrs of Jesus. I saw a beast carrying the woman and those who will "MARVEL"; whose names were not written in the Book of Life from when the world began. There are kings and kingdoms who will give their power to this beast. They are working together and will make war with the Lamb and the Lamb will overcome them. He is Lord of lords and King of kings. Beware of the Goat and the goats for the bible describes their rebellion against right and God's divine will. Jesus in the day will have His Holy Angels with Him, and separate the Goats from the sheep. The sheep will be placed at His right hand and the goats at His left. The sheep will enter into eternal life, joy and peace, but the goats will be cast into outer darkness and damnation along with Satan and his followers; there will be wailing and gnashing of teeth (Matthew 25:31-46). Who are you following and where are they leading you? Be careful to not allow people to make you proud to be called a GOAT. Beware of the goats and wolves!

The water where the Harlot sits have peoples, multitudes, nations (many races), and tongues (many languages). The beast had ten horns and these represent the nations who hate the harlot, and make her desolate, and naked, eat her flesh and burn her. For God has put in their hearts to fulfill His purpose, to be of one mind, and to give their kingdom to the beast, until the words of God are fulfilled. And the woman whom you saw is that great city that reigns over kings of the earth.

After these things I saw another angel coming down from heaven, having great authority, and the earth was illuminated with his glory. And he cried mightily with a loud voice, saying, "Babylon the great is fallen, and has become a dwelling place of demons, a prison for every foul spirit, and a gage for every unclean and hateful bird. For all the nations have drunk of the wine of the wrath of her fornication, the kings of the earth have committed fornication with her, and the merchants-business men have become rich through the abundance of her luxury."

And I heard another voice from heaven saying, "Come out of her, my people, lest you receive of her plaques. For her sins have reached to heaven, and God has remembered her iniquities. Render to her just as she rendered to you, and repay her double according to her works; in the cup which she has mixed, mix double for her." In the measure that she glorified herself and lived luxuriously, in the same measure give her torment and sorrow; for she says in her heart, "I sit a queen, and will not see sorrow." Therefore, her plagues will come in one day—death and mourning and famine. And she will be utterly burned with fire, for strong is the Lord God who judges her. The world will mourn her fall. The kings of the earth who committed fornication and lived luxuriously with her will weep and lament for her when they see the smoke of her burning, standing at a distance for fear of her torment, saying, "Atlas, alas, that great nation Babylon, that mighty nation! For in one hour, sixty minutes (60 years) your judgment has come." The businessmen of the world will weep and mourn over her, since no one will buy their cargo anymore; they have no one to buy their merchandise because she is gone. The fruit that your soul longed for, even the souls of men, are gone from you, and all the things that are rich and splendid have gone from you, and will find them no more in you at all. The merchants and businesses owners of these things, who became rich by her, will stand at a distance for fear of her torment, weeping and wailing, and saying, "Atlas, alas, that great nation that was clothed in fine linen, purple, and scarlet, and adorned with gold and precious stones and pearls! For in one hour such great riches came to nothing." Every ship-master, all who travel by ship and trade cargo, sailors, airplanes, pilots, trucks, and as many who trade by sea and air, stood at a distance and cried out when they saw the smoke of her burning, saying, "Who is like this great nation?"

They threw dust on their heads and cried out, weeping and wailing, and saying, "Atlas, alas, that great nation, in which all who had ships and planes who traded with her cried as they saw the smoke of her burning, 'What nation was like the great Nation?'"

Great and powerful people all around the world watch her burn in disbelief. This news is everywhere at one time. Every device, and the INTERNET is crashing. We have never seen men of all races and languages crying over her, even her enemies because she fed their families and made them rich, granting them all kinds of opportunities. For in a single hour she has been laid waste. "Rejoice over her, O heaven, and you saints and apostles and prophets, for God has given judgment for you against her!"

Then, a mighty angel took up a stone like a great millstone and threw it into the sea, saying, "So will Babylon the great city be thrown down with violence, and will be found no more; and the sound of music, the club and musicians will be heard in you no more, and the sound of building and any skill be found in you no more, the lights will go out and never seen in you again, no more voice of the groom and bride, no more weddings will be heard in you, for the businessmen and traders were the great ones of the earth. All nations were deceived by your sorcery. And in her was found the blood of the prophets and saints, anyone who tried to warn her of her sins were slain in her streets, hung and abused, murdered with no justice in sight. In her is the blood of all the prophets and saints because she is a nation of all people from around the world, God saw fit to do it this way. Judging a nation who laid hands on His prophets around the world."

After this I heard what seemed to be the loud voice of a great multitude in heaven, crying out, "Hallelujah! Salvation and glory and power belong to our God, for judgments are true and just; for he has judged the prostitute who corrupted the earth with her immorality, and avenged on her blood of his servants." Those who have no power to defend themselves, God has you. He's not weak but patient and merciful, but she will not repent even when God was quiet while she went wild! Once more they cried out, "Hallelujah! The smoke from her goes up forever and ever." And the twenty-four elders and the four living creatures fell down and worshiped God who was seated on the throne, saying, "Amen. Hallelujah!" And from the throne came a voice saying, "Praise our God, all you his servants, you who fear him, small and great." Then I heard what seemed like the roar of many waters and like the sound of mighty peals of thunder, crying out, "Hallelujah! For the Lord our God the Almighty reigns. Let us rejoice and exult and give him glory, for the marriage of the Lamb has come, and his Bride has made herself ready; it was granted her to clothe herself with fine linen, bright and pure"—for the linen is the righteous deeds of the saints. And the angel said to me, "Write this: Blessed are those who are invited to the marriage supper of the Lamb." And he said to me, "These are true words of God." Then I fell down at his feet to worship him, but he said to me, "You must not do that! I am a fellow servant with you and your brothers who hold the testimony of Jesus. Worship God." For the testimony of Jesus is the spirit of prophecy.

As believers and Christians we are so wrong to say, "Rest in peace!" Can't we see this is two beings from different worlds having a conversation and clearly the angel is saying I'm a servant with you? You are a witness and have been chosen to write these things for the future church that they may believe when these things come to pass. John saw over 2,000 years ago technology that was unexplainable. For example, the whole world would see the city burning at one time. The entire world would see at the same time. How?! He could not explain it. People, for centuries, thought this was ridiculous. But this generation is a witness of seeing things around the world through INTERNET; social media is a normal thing for us.

JESUS IS REAL! HEAVEN IS REAL! HELL IS REAL! LIFE AFTER DEATH IS REAL! DO YOU HEAR THE DUOLOGUE OF JOHN AND THE ANGEL? THE ANGEL IS FROM ETERNITY HAVING A CONVERSATION WITH JOHN WHO IS IN THE EARTH. THE ANGEL IS GIVEN AN ACCOUNT OF THOSE THAT HAVE PASSED ON TO HEAVEN BUT GOD HAS NOT FORGOTTEN HOW THEY WERE TREATED AND DIED WHILE IN TIME. HIS VENGEANCE IS ON THE BLOODLINE OF THOSE WHO HAVE PASSED ON AND ARE IN HELL (JAIL IN ETERNITY AWAITING THEIR COURT DATE) WHILE THEIR DESCENDANTS ARE STILL RAISING HELL ON EARTH, DECEIVED IN THINKING THERE IS NO ACCOUNTABILITY OR JUDGMENT.

THEY REALLY BOUGHT INTO THE LIE OF THE
DEVIL, THAT THEIR FOLKS ARE RESTING IN PEACE!
THERE ARE DIFFERENT PARTS OF HELL LIKE THERE
ARE DIFFERENT PARTS OF ANY MAJOR JAIL-HOUSE
IN AMERICA.

There are innumerable people who wish they could get a
pass like the angel who was John's messenger to come to the
earth to warn their family and friends of the place they are in.
Rules; no visitors! If you take your last breath and find yourself being booked in, you can kiss your behind goodbye and
good riddance! Once you are assigned to your holding place,
you have to wait for your official court date to stand before
the "Just Judge" and His White Throne. The true Supreme
Court! He's going to make our courts look like a kindergarten
playroom. The true Supreme Court ruled by the One TRUE
Supreme God Almighty!

In this generation we are witnessing a shift in the entire
world. There's a desperate need for change and great expectations in hopes for better. God has been sort of quiet from 1619
to 2019...four hundred years. I've learned God's ways are truly
not like ours. Ten generations God has been receiving His
people, or should I say children. It's like the earth was in labor
pains giving birth to many babies. Despite all of the pain and
heartaches those saints went straight home with their Heavenly Father. Many will be surprised when they die and take
their last breath here on earth, and then open their eyes on
the other side and none of us can take our skin color with
us! Another lie spun by the devil! You take your soul, your
heart, and receive a new body (house). Whatever you hate the
most in earth if you go to hell is what you find yourself in

while waiting to go to trial. If you hate white people, you will be confined to white skin, you will have a mirror in your cell that can't be broken. If you hate black people, you will find yourself trapped in black skin until you go to court for trial. Everything you ever did that's unrepentant is SIN! And will be played in that court and you will have witnesses from your time in the earth to testify of your actions. Those who were murdered and abused will be in court like Jesus. Meaning after his death and resurrection He kept the five holes put in His body on purpose as evidence, but it won't hurt anymore. It will be your day in court that you were denied in the earth because of unfair treatment and a system against you. Cases will be judged, but more importantly the heart will be on trial. That is why repentance is so important. Jesus gave us an out! A plea bargain. Take the deal! Just repent while you have time and a chance! Repentance is a guilty plea but in exchange having all charges dropped... case dismissed!

God is the One who put Mr. Donald Trump in for president for the time he was in office. It was shocking to a lot of people when he won, many believed then it was voters' fraud. But God used this man to bring out things in America and Americans that we thought we had overcome. God put Donald Trump in office as chief and commander to wake America up! The freedoms that many of us took for granted all of a sudden have become so fragile. How about the freedom of going to the store without masks? Sending our children to school or even going to work, or waking up and taking a walk in the park on the weekend? How about just going to the gym for a workout? When restaurants and shopping malls closed, we were done, and then vacations and traveling were banned or mandated restrictions. Now we cannot go to church or to football games. Holidays became lonely days, trying to figure out how to be social, loving, and safe. We took so many values for granted, complained about almost everything, and missed what was most important. Everyone has been affected by this presidency and we are not out of hot water as of yet. It took a person who was not a politician to break the mold of this country and expose hypocrisy. He was and is not politically correct by a long shot. 20/20 means perfect vision, well God used the year 2020 to correct our vision as a nation. To put on our spiritual glasses only to find out how much we have not been seeing. I call 2020 the year of corrective vision. Just because we didn't see it doesn't mean it wasn't there. We are so divided by so many things. "A divided house cannot stand." Jesus said this. He also said, "If Satan cast out Satan than his kingdom is divided and it cannot stand." Well, we have seen for the first time in our lifetime, Satan casting out Satan! This country is divided almost in half. The people have spoken. God allowed these things to happen for the end time prophecy. COVID-19 is a tragedy for us as a country, especially with over 600,000 American lives lost. To those who made it to heaven, trust and believe now they don't ever want to come back. The world watches us to see how we will handle all of this. We need to admit that we need God's help. Even with a cure for COVID-19 where is the cure for hate? Where is the answer for our Capital? We have so many problems not just in America but around the world. We as the church should repent first and show the world how we suffered from a little blindness just like the Pharisees. Judgment starts at the household of faith. We are supposed to be the examples for kingdom and righteousness rooted in love. What's sad is we have undercover evangelicals who are more political than kingdom and righteousness. We were having church, but harboring hate and division. Where is the church? Twelve men turned this world upside down because they weren't playing politics or church; they were kingdom-minded, understanding that no matter how many years we are on this earth we are going to give an account for what we say, not say, and what's in our hearts. No heart can hide from God. "The way of the hypocrite will perish." Well, guess what? It's perishing because we are letting it all hang out.

If we want true healing, we have to have dialog and stop pretending we had nothing to do with the past. I hear talk of REVIVAL—there's no possibility of revival without RE-PENTANCE! God is just! We can no longer hide behind nice clothes, cars, houses, money, and eating while heaven is in an uproar! God is showing us that our time is up for being politically correct or hypocrites like the Pharisees. God even shut down the churches to get the pastors' attentions and some are still using social media to show off vanity! Some pastors' and religious leaders' social media accounts will testify against them in God's court just like those who penetrated the Capital. God is trying to tell us more than something! I will say it, "REPENT!"

Jeremiah would not be trying to be everybody's friend while putting him and God on the outs! This makes me believe that just because we attend church, doesn't mean we are the church and definitely not kingdom. Jesus told us to preach the gospel of the kingdom. We are supposed to be the conduit in which the kingdom is supposed to come through. When it

comes to politics we set Jesus to the side to support our political parties, but I say we need the Lord with us to pray for
them and be an example. But we have too many pastors and
leaders who are brown-nosing and worshiping the president.
How can he get help if the prophets are not honest? Prophets
anointed kings, now we have prophets who want to take pictures with the president rather than fasting and praying to
get a true word to our leaders in Washington and across this
great nation as we call it! If you love God and your country,
then we better step it up and get ourselves together because
our enemies are not going to help us fix it or heal! As a nation and people, we need to turn back to God and admit we
need His help and we are wrong, in and out of the church.
God used Joseph to save both the church and the world. They
both needed saving and so do we!

Apostle Paul would not have time for foolishness, and this
is why his writings are what they are because the church was
losing it even in his day and time. Pastors are selling their
crowns for followers, going out to eat, clothes, titles and attention... and selfies. Who would have believed this was just
60 years ago? The people who sacrificed so much for us would
not believe what had happened to our nation. How could we
go backwards? How can we call ourselves a God-fearing nation and be so hateful? Something has happened to us. "We
have a form of godliness, but deny the power." The power is
love. What happened to us? Everyone tells us what we want
to hear but the true conversations are the ones happening behind closed doors after work, and after church, especially after worship service. How can a whole new generation carry
such hate? How can we say we love God and hate our brothers

and sisters because of skin color or sexual preference or denomination? America was born from desperation of needing God. She didn't start out beautiful at all. No one wanted to be her in the beginning. The reality is, the world didn't think she would last as long as she did in this strange place, this unfamiliar land. She was so humble in the beginning. America the Beautiful, where are you? So even in church we are politically correct by tolerating one another when our Lord commands us to love one another. If we hate each other in time, then we definitely will hate each other in eternity. This is why God will separate us ultimately and it will not be by the color of our skin, but the content of our character. It's what we're hiding that God is going to Judge. It's those words we speak that we think no one outside of our little circles will ever hear, that's what God will play in His courtroom on that day. When she established her first independence, she honored God with her money. "In God We Trust" is on the back of her first dollar bill. Without God she would be nothing. The odds were always stacked against her through wars, disease, sickness, hate, and enemy plots globally. It was no doubt that it's God who helped her stand still and thrive as a world leader.

We must recognize the end of an era. When an era comes to its end there's nothing to do but change and get in front of the new era and by God don't try to stop progress, because if so, you will find yourself on the wrong end of change and be left behind. It's hard when you have done things a certain way for so long, but too long can be dangerous. Things are always changing. We need to have the discernment to see change coming and be strategic to win. We want to be allies with progress, not the enemy. There was a time when horses and buggies were the most common mode of transportation. It was the time and era for the horse and anyone who was busy surrounded the horse, from blacksmiths, horseshoes, saddles, etc. But when the car came on the seen the era for the horse as the primary mode of transportation was coming to its end. For those in the horse and buggy business saw the car as the enemy or threat, fought its progress and arrival on their scene. As inevitable as it was for the era of the horse to come to its end, those who were in the business saw it as though they were coming to an end. The horse did not come to an end neither did the people who had horses but the commerce did and the value of the horse for trade did, so the smart thing to do would be to embrace the inevitable change on the verge of dominance; which is the automobile.

The easy thing to do is to get those who own horses and/ or was in the horse business to make cars and car makers their enemy. In the beginning you will have more people for the way things used to be rather than where things are going. Change is inevitable, whether good or bad. You have those who fight a losing battle and most times are stubborn and ig- norant to the truth and die miserably trying to be God and can't live long enough to see they have lost the battle. But we have those who believe they can stop it rather than becoming a part of it. What's remarkably amazing about life is no one gets to stay here forever. So if it's good, why not be a part of greatness? It is challenging to let go of the past that has been good or great to someone. But sometimes greatness for one person is misery for another. The horse owners may have been horrified of the automobile era, but if the horse could talk he would probably say, "Thank you, Lord! Now we are free to do other things, anything but the burden we have for so long carried." Where change may be horrifying to the one group, it is more than welcome to another. Nonetheless, they fought the coming of the automobile era tooth and nail only to learn from history that their children not only would purchase and drive an automobile, but apply for a job to build them. Families are fighting over children choosing change for the future while the owners of horses are feeling betrayed by their own blood. This is not a betrayal, this is life. The previous generations who were the best at raising and training horses, their children had become the best car makers, mechanics, and engineers. In the end how many people were fighting for the horse to be the glory of our transportation?

There are so many history lessons we have that showcase the end of an era. It's monumental for humanity when people sacrifice to make our world a better place to live in harmony and unity. We should welcome change if it's for a nation to achieve greatness. Through inventions and discoveries, we as a nation are known around the world for greatness. We are at the cusp of a new era of "Making America Greater" not just "Make America Great" again! If we truly believe in "Make America Great Again" then we must turn back to the God who made her Great in the first place. How can we "Make America Great Again" without the God who made her Great? Our God is a progressive God and if you are not for progress then you are not for God. Blessings is to "add to" or multiply," meaning God adds to our lives. Satan, on the other hand, "divides and subtracts" from our lives. The devil is the god of division. We need to embrace what made us "Great," and be honest about what made us not so great as a nation. Division is our enemy that need not to be glorified. Unity is our friend, the power and strength that lifts us above our adversaries. Our wise leaders of yesterday could see far into the future when they named us, "The United States of America." This is the STAMP on our first currency, the one-dollar bill. It is the mark of who we are. Look at the one dollar and see the divine vision of our Forefathers. They understood something we are taking for granted. United we stand and divided we fall. Also on the back of the dollar is, "IN GOD WE TRUST." These things are on purpose for a greater purpose than the era they were written, but for a far greater America than the one they were living in when they pasted the bill for our first One Dollar Bill. The Great Seal on the reverse side of our dollar motto is, Annuit Coeptis, which is Latin for, "God has approved our undertakings" or "God has favored us." If we allow anyone to remove God from us they will without a doubt remove God's favor that is on America. The second motto is, "Novus Ordo Seclorum," which is Latin for, "A New Order of the Ages (is born)." In a nutshell, "The End of an Era." Another motto on the other Great Seal reads, "E Pluribus Unum," from the Great Seal of the United States of America, and it means, "Out of many, One." This comes from the writings of Cicero who said, "When each person loves the other as much as himself, it makes one out of many." This is our pledge for "Unity" once again. Many states acting as One nation is our very foundation to the establishing of this Great Nation we've come to love, "The United States of America." If we love our country, we must know that it's very survival depends upon our willingness and determination to unite us rather than divide us.

We are finding more reasons to be defined as, "The Divided States of America."

"Jesus knew their thoughts and said to them, "Any kingdom divided against itself will be ruined, and a house divided against itself will fall." (Luke 11:17)

If we say we love our country, then we must get to the root of what divides us and start our healing process to be united. How much longer can we stand being divided? The devil is not going to wait for us Americans to figure it out! And we need to fix things between us and our God who blessed us in the first place. Without God's favor the world will not have a reason to respect or fear us. The devil's always looking for a way to infiltrate. Let's not make it so easy for him by assisting him and justifying it.

The founding fathers of this nation didn't by far proclaim to be perfect, but what they did exemplify is the willingness to acknowledge God in taking their next steps for change. They were humble enough to know that without God they would have lost many battles as well as wars. Their wins against more established and powerful nations at the time of the first dollar gave them the inspiration for their seal. They did not see it at the time, but believed God by faith for a greater reason. This seal would ultimately become the "Great Seal;" the greatest symbol of power in the modern world. The leaders of this Great Nation did not see it with their eyes, they saw it by faith in God. This same God who has blessed, empowered, protected, and provided for them, and brought them up out of impossible situations where they knew it was by divine intervention they came out alive. God promised them if they kept Him first he would make them Great! How can "America Be Great Again" if she abandons God and the principles from which she was established?

As leaders of the modern world, we have the ability to see our mistakes, learn from them, and make the necessary adjustments to bring about change. To save a nation we must have a proper assessment. No, we were not perfect, but favored. We must in turn, learn from our mistakes, not repeat them or attempt to resurrect them. What worked yesterday will not work today. People have changed...times have changed, and we must with a moral compass change for the better.

If America is to remain, "America The Beautiful" then she must rid herself of the ugliness of hate, racism, bigotry, sexism, and the lawlessness that offends God. Somebody had a visit from God and it was made crystal clear that the way this country started was not the way it would finish. God always used great leaders to bring about change who are not intimidated by those who oppose the better good.

Listen to what God says in His word concerning leaders and government; *"Let every person be subject to the governing authorities. For there is no authority except from God, and those that exist has been instituted by God. Therefore, whoever resists the authorities resists what God has appointed, and those who resists will incur judgment. For rulers are not a terror to good conduct, but bad. Would you have no fear of the one who is in authority? Then do what is good, and you will receive his approval, for he is God's servant for good. But if you do wrong, be afraid, for he does not bear his weapon in vain. For he is the servant of God, an avenger who carries out God's wrath on the wrongdoer. Therefore, one must be in subjection, not only to avoid God's wrath but also for the sake of conscience."*

This is why Dr. Martin Luther King did "non-violent protests" because he was directed by God on how to handle these demonstrations. He understood very clearly that the leaders were to be accountable to God for how they handle citizens and the law. So, for the leaders who abused their authority, there is NO "Rest in peace" for any of them who killed and abused. They are on the other side of life, an eternity in Hell (jail of the afterlife awaiting trial); no one gets away with anything. God is the true Judge. Whether we like who's in office or not, God placed them there. Good or evil, God will judge them all and pay them according to how they treated His people in time.

When the era for **slavery** had come to an end, God used his servant, Abraham Lincoln, to issue the Emancipation Proclamation in 1863. Why? Because the era for **slavery** had come to an end. Slavery now had become an issue for God and men. The Proclamation itself freed very little slaves, but it was the death knell for slavery (the hint of the ending of an era) in the United States. Eventually, the Emancipation Proclamation led to the proposal and ratification of the Thirteenth Amendment to the Constitution, which formally abolished slavery. It's not by chance it was the Thirteenth Amendment, because thirteen means, "The Highest Possible Spiritual Number." Look on the back of the dollar bill and you will find signs and symbols of "13" everywhere. America did not become established as a nation until it had 13 colonies. Think this to be by chance? No way! God is in control!

1865 to 1965 were one hundred years of not letting the

slaves completely go, although the law said so, because one group saw them as slaves while on the other hand, God saw them as sons. When the era of slavery was over in Egypt, Pharaoh felt the slaves belonged to him. When he decided not to let them go after 400 years, he started a fight with God. Well, we know who won. When the end of that era came to an end, then Pharaoh didn't stand a chance in this fight. Because he was so powerful over the Hebrews for so long, he really thought it was because of his power. But not so, God made a promise to Abraham that his seed would be in bondage for 400 years and after that period was up (end of an era), He would deliver them and keep His promise to Abraham; this was God's covenant to him. As long as God kept silent for 400 years Pharaoh was in charge, but when God sent His servant Moses to tell Pharaoh to let His people go, every day he kept them in bondage he was in violation with God Almighty.

In August of 1619, a ship with 20 captives landed at Point Comfort in Virginia, ushering in the era of American slavery. In 1865 President Abraham Lincoln used his God-given authority here on earth to free the slaves; it cost him his life. "We will visit the Holy Land and see those places hallowed by the footsteps of the Savior," the president said. "There is no place I so much desire to see as Jerusalem." These, then, are the final words of Abraham Lincoln in this world. The Civil Rights Act of 1964 was first proposed by President John F. Kennedy, but it was signed by his successor, Lyndon B. Johnson. This took one hundred years to get done—Civil War, the life of two presidents in particular, and countless lives. So this journey has been 400 years long, August of 2019 brought us up to-date of 400 years since this journey began. Four hundred years of God's grace. The year 2019 marked the end of an era. The year 2020 is the first year of a new era. 2020 is God's 20/20, the year to show us how much we need corrective vision, to make it possible to see our history through the eyes of God. The year 2020 came in with a bang. We wanted 2020 to go away for a new year to come in, but 2021 came in with another historic bang! Year number two of the new era. January 6, 2021 the attack on our Nation's Capital is going down in our nation's history not as a glorious day, but of sin and shame. Who could have imagined? Why? It's divine! It's spiritual! Just like how COVID-19 is real but we can't see it, God is real but we can't see Him, yet we see the effects. Believe it, we have entered into a new era and God's grace is running out because of our arrogance and pride. So many American lives lost and not just this country but around the world. The last time the world was brought together for any tragedy on this scale, it ended with a World War. We must see the signs and not try to escape from the truth. Coronavirus is the beginning of a World War with an enemy that we cannot see, who is against humanity. The call to defeat this enemy is unity and not division. We all need divine wisdom, but our leaders would need to humble themselves and admit we need God's help on this one. Since men can't get it right, don't want to humble themselves, and pray and seek God's face, will it take the woman to do it?

But now, she must be heard loud and clear through her own voice! She has to be brought to the light to help fix this problem the world is having. It's going to take all the women of the world to fix the problems we've got around the world; it needs to be a global effort! The serpent targeted the woman from the beginning and she will be heard in the end! If those who oppose evil will not give her a platform to be heard, the serpent surely will. When the church told her to be quiet, the world gave her a horn! Should we, who say we are the leaders of God, give her the right to be heard, since in the scriptures, we see how the enemy hates her? We are to teach and protect her. We are not controlling her, but assisting her as guiding lights in this dark world. Again, I'm not empowering the serpent in the woman, but the God in her; there is a difference. When a woman is faithfully working to bring good to any situation, she should be heard, supported, and confident. Are we hypocrites, afraid of change? We will use her for evil, but we need her input for good, we need her for change. The earth will listen to her; the Word of God says so. "And the earth helped the woman and swallowed up the flood, that the serpent sent, to carry the woman away." All creations are in pain, waiting for the woman to be revealed. Women are working overtime on their outer appearance, and not investing much into the heart. She can't fulfill her purpose carrying all of that hurt and pain! We are encouraging her to be vain; "eye candy!" But she's more than that! What she has on the inside is power; intellectual. Maybe we are partially responsible by denying her as a voice. She has to be heard one way or another; this is who she is, and we need to take more time to know her.

"America The Beautiful" is just what she is when she's focused on who made her beautiful.

God's grace was on her before. Could it be that His grace is on her if she takes the wheel with Him as the captain? God showed a woman named Katherine Lee Bates in 1893 the beauty of this country although bigotry and hate was standing in her way. She wrote this poem, which later was turned into a song along with Samuel A. Ward. Traveling by train and looking out of the window, she wrote what was inspired by God's creation. Although America was far from perfect, this inspired work had words of hope. Somewhat past, present, and futuristic at the same time, here is "America The Beautiful:"

"O beautiful for spacious skies, for amber ways of grain, for purple mountain majesties Above the fruited plain!
America! America! God shed His grace on thee, and crown thy good with brotherhood, from sea to shining sea." (from the Atlantic Ocean to the Pacific Ocean)
God is still waiting on America to live up to what he gave to her in these words."

The woman is famously known for being made from the man's rib, but in heaven she is known by being created from God's heart. She represents God's glory. This is why she has so many enemies with and without prejudice. Your enemy will do anything to make her feel insecure, all the while he knows he cannot get the job done without her. He will do anything for her not to lead. She can assist with boundaries and restrictions but has no freedom to bring her solutions and resolve. He will give her trinkets of success but not the whole gamete. In the premature end, God, her maker, will give her a chance to make things right with God and man while giving her the revenge she was unable to give herself. The revenge is not to destroy her enemy, but show him what leading looks like when God is at the helm. God will be her protector and guide. He will give her wisdom to lead. He's not putting her in powerful roles and positions to destroy, but to save. Be wise in this time and season to understand the same enemy that tripped you up in the garden is still in beautiful places waiting on his opportunity to use you against the One who created you for His purpose. Your enemy knows you are his replacement, God's revision to His own blueprint for life. God is the writer, producer, and director to this movie called, "Life" and the woman is the leading role and the story does not end with her in fear or bondage but in victory and sitting upon her throne provided by God himself. This movement cannot be stopped! Look at how far she has come in the past 100 years. Take a look back at her oppositions and what she achieved in spite of. She must know this, and pursue on purpose, with her destiny in mind. She must know God put her in a position and place of power. She must use her authority to compel her people and nation to repent and turn back to her (America's) God. Her ONE who is the real reason why she was GREAT!

We say, "We love our country, we love America." It's a beautiful place, yes it is, but how can we love America and not its citizens? God commands that we love one another. Most of our problems in America are because we are bankrupted in love. Who is America without the diversities of people not found in all of the world? America is Beautiful because of the mixes and differences of people found in no other nation. That's what makes America, America—all the many races of people from around the world found in this one place. "Many together as one."

"America The Beautiful!"

www.ingramcontent.com/pod-product-compliance
Lightning Source LLC
Chambersburg PA
CBHW021953090426
42811CB00001B/3